CAMBRIDGE
UNIVERSITY PRESS

IB English A
Language and Literature

EXAM PREPARATION AND PRACTICE

David James

Nic Amy

David McIntyre

DEDICATED TEACHER AWARDS

Teachers play an important part in shaping futures.
Our Dedicated Teacher Awards recognise the hard
work that teachers put in every day.

Thank you to everyone who nominated this year; we have been inspired and moved
by all of your stories. Well done to all of our nominees for your dedication to learning
and for inspiring the next generation of thinkers, leaders and innovators.

Congratulations to our incredible winner and finalists!

WINNER

Patricia Abril
Cambridge School,
Colombia

Stanley Manaay
Salvacion National High School,
Philippines

Tiffany Cavanagh
Trident College Solwezi,
Zambia

Helen Comerford
Lumen Christi Catholic College,
Australia

John Nicko Coyoca
University of San Jose-Recoletos,
Philippines

Meera Rangarajan
RBK International Academy,
India

For more information about our dedicated teachers and their stories, go to
dedicatedteacher.cambridge.org

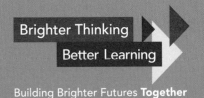

Brighter Thinking
Better Learning

Building Brighter Futures **Together**

CAMBRIDGE
UNIVERSITY PRESS

University Printing House, Cambridge CB2 8BS, United Kingdom

One Liberty Plaza, 20th Floor, New York, NY 10006, USA

477 Williamstown Road, Port Melbourne, VIC 3207, Australia

314–321, 3rd Floor, Plot 3, Splendor Forum, Jasola District Centre, New Delhi – 110025, India

79 Anson Road, #06–04/06, Singapore 079906

Cambridge University Press is part of the University of Cambridge.
It furthers the University's mission by disseminating knowledge in the pursuit of
education, learning and research at the highest international levels of excellence.

www.cambridge.org
Information on this title: www.cambridge.org/9781108704960

First published 2020

20 19 18 17 16 15 14 13 12 11 10 9 8 7 6 5 4 3 2 1

Printed in Italy by L.E.G.O. S.p.A.

A catalogue record for this publication is available from the British Library

ISBN 978-1-108-70496-0

Additional resources for this publication at cambridge.org/9781108704960

Cambridge University Press has no responsibility for the persistence or accuracy
of URLs for external or third-party internet websites referred to in this publication,
and does not guarantee that any content on such websites is, or will remain,
accurate or appropriate. Information regarding prices, travel timetables, and other
factual information given in this work is correct at the time of first printing but
Cambridge University Press does not guarantee the accuracy of such information
thereafter.

....

Contents

Introduction

In this section you will:

- learn about the features in this book and how to use them
- gain an overview of the English A: Language and Literature course
- become familiar with the aims and assessment objectives for the course
- find out the format and requirements for the different course assessments
- find guidance on how to use the learner portfolio effectively
- learn how the literary works and non-literary texts you will study in your course are selected
- become familiar with the key command terms for your study of language and literature.

How to use this book

Paper 1

A 'Getting started' task will engage you with the theme of the unit and uncover what you already know

Texts cover a range of international contexts

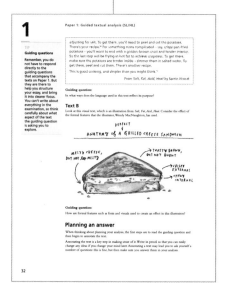

In this section you will explore a variety of different text types

Clear learning objectives for each section

The assessment and evaluation criteria are clearly summarised for each component

Paper 2

You will be encouraged to evaluate sample student responses

You will write and assess your own draft responses

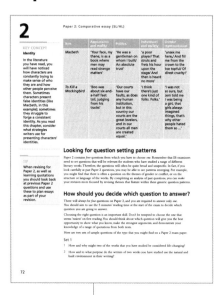

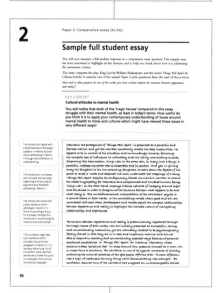

This section refers to the seven key concepts

You will be asked to assign sample responses with a grade

You will develop your editing and redrafting skills

Higher-level essay

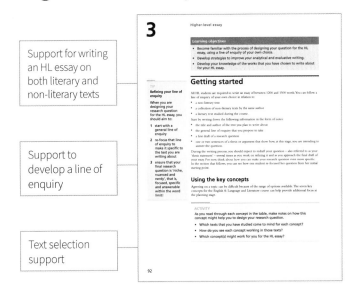

Support for writing an HL essay on both literary and non-literary texts

Support to develop a line of enquiry

Text selection support

An emphasis on international mindedness throughout

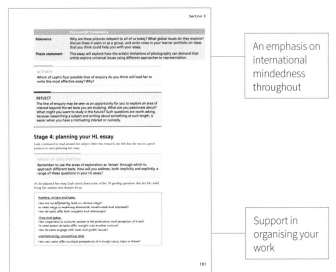

Support in organising your work

Individual oral

Develop skills for both analysis and discussion

Understand how to talk about a body of work

Organised around the five global issues

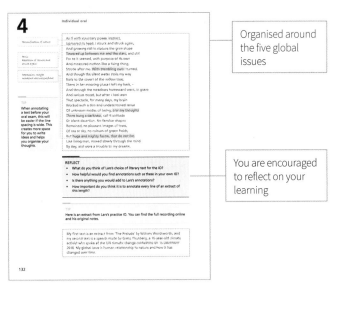

You are encouraged to reflect on your learning

Exam strategy training tips can be found throughout the book

Practice papers

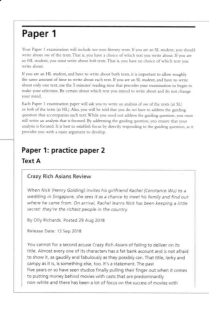

Two practice papers to help you prepare for the exam

Sample HL essays and assessment criteria

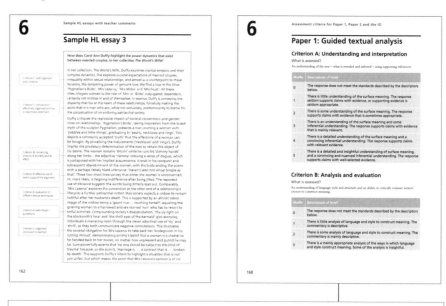

Mark schemes and assessment criteria can be referred to regularly, to ensure that you understand the required standard

Introduction to the English A: Language and Literature course

IB English A: Language and Literature – syllabus overview

This book will help you prepare and practise for your IB English A: Language and Literature examinations. The different assessment components will test what you have learnt and understood during the course. In preparing for these examinations, it is therefore essential to understand what you will learn during your course of study. Think of the assessment as the end point of your learning – an important part of your course, rather than something separate from it.

This introductory section will outline what you will be studying and learning during your course.

How your course is structured

Your course will involve equal study of both literature and language texts. At times, you may want to separate your study of literary works and language texts. At other times, and perhaps more frequently, it may be more interesting and productive to think about both literary works and language texts as examples of 'language in use', where language can be thought of as both practical and aesthetic, often at the same time.

Language is a principal vehicle for human communication. In important ways, it both reflects and shapes how we experience the world. That makes it so interesting and valuable to study! Studying language and literature becomes the study of a significant aspect of human existence. During your course, you will:

- critically consider language texts and literary works
- be encouraged to develop and motivate your own understanding of language and literature
- have your perspective challenged by considering alternative viewpoints
- read closely and for detail, considering the different ways that writers' choices, text types, literary forms and context influence meaning
- learn that texts and literary works do not speak for themselves, but rather can be understood in a variety of ways.

In addition to analysing language and literature, including texts that may contain audio and visual elements, you will be asked to write and produce your own texts. This creative work will, in turn, help you understand the imaginative work of others.

The course sets out to teach ideas such as these, and assesses your understanding and skills of this nature. As you approach your study and examinations, it is helpful to bear in mind the close relationship between what is taught and what is assessed.

This book is intended to supplement your classroom study, and to guide you towards success in examinations through support and activities that develop your skills and understanding. While the book can help you to enhance your potential to do well in examinations, it is not an alternative to the focused and sustained study that your course requires!

Course requirements

Literary works

Some parts of your course involve the study of language, some the study of literature, and some the study of both at the same time. The examinations reflect this: some assess your understanding of *either* language *or* literature, and others your understanding of both language *and* literature. As you develop your understanding of the course and its assessment, it is important to remember whether you are being assessed on your understanding of literary works, non-literary texts or both.

You will study a wide range of literary works, and your understanding of these will be assessed both during and at the end of your course. Your teacher will choose the literary works you study, and these choices must adhere to the IB regulations. Your teacher may involve you in this choice. While IB regulations allow flexibility of choice, they ensure that all students study a variety of literary forms from different places and times. The number of literary works you study will depend on whether you are a higher-level (HL) or a standard-level (SL) student.

- HL students will study *six* literary works. At least *two* of these will be in translation (i.e. translated from a language other than English).

- SL students will study *four* literary works. At least *one* of these will be in translation (i.e. translated from a language other than English).

The literary forms you will study in your course will be taken from the following:

- prose: fiction (e.g. novels)

- prose: non-fiction (e.g. travel writing)

- drama

- poetry.

Non-literary texts

The course gives equal weight to the study of language and literature. Half of your study will focus on the study of literary works, and the other half will focus on the study of non-literary texts. The kinds of non-literary text you study will be very wide-ranging, and may include:

- blogs

- electronic texts

- reports

- photographs

- magazine articles.

In the same way that your literary works will be chosen to represent different places, times and voices, non-literary texts will be chosen to represent diversity through time and space.

At times, a literary work can be very different from a non-literary text, in terms of language, form and function. At other times, these differences may be much less obvious, and it may become challenging to differentiate between the literary and the non-literary. However, you should see this challenge as a positive one: remember that literary and non-literary texts often share much in common – this can help you as you approach your examinations. For example, novels are normally regarded as literary works, while newspaper stories are not. However, newspaper stories may contain language features that are frequently regarded as literary. Remember that the distinction between literary and non-literary texts is not absolute; this will help you find coherence in your studies and build all the skills needed for success in your course.

In some cases, you will study 'discrete' non-literary texts, or texts that are part of a wider 'body of work'. If, for example, you study one photograph, this is an example of 'discrete' study: by contrast, if you study 15 photographs taken by the *same* photographer, this is an example of a 'body of work'. In both cases, your study of non-literary texts is intended to increase your understanding of the different ways that texts establish meaning and effect.

It is important to remember that only those texts studied as part of a wider 'body of work' may be used for the individual oral (IO) examination and, for some students, the higher-level (HL) essay.

How your course is organised

There is no single way for teachers to organise your course of study. Teachers will organise courses differently, including the selection of literary works and non-literary texts, depending on a variety of factors that reflect the student population, and the social and cultural circumstances of your school. Teachers are given a good degree of freedom to construct interesting and engaging courses, but they must also adhere to IB regulations. They are guided by the five key organising principles (areas of exploration, concepts, theory of knowledge, approaches to learning, and accountability) discussed in the rest of this subsection.

Areas of exploration

There are three areas of exploration:

- readers, writers, texts

- time and space

- intertextuality – connecting texts.

Teachers can decide how to build these areas of exploration into your course of study. Broadly speaking, the areas of exploration should inform the teaching of all the texts that you study, whether literary or non-literary, and each area of exploration should be given equal attention in your course as a whole. At times, your teacher may focus on one area of exploration and give less attention to the others.

It is important to understand that these areas of exploration are not directly assessed. However, they do provide you with a useful 'thinking tool' around which you can develop your ideas, expand your understanding and make connections across your course.

What does each area of exploration mean?

Readers, writers, texts

This area of exploration emphasises the *textual*. It involves the close study of language and structure, including the choices that writers make.

Time and space

This area of exploration emphasises the *contextual*. Writers and readers are influenced by the time and place in which they write or read, and contextual factors include the social, cultural, economic, political and personal circumstances that may influence the choices that writers (and publishers) make, and the ways in which texts are read and understood.

Intertextuality – connecting texts

This final area of exploration emphasises the *intertextual*; that is, the relationships that exist between literary works or texts. For example, it is possible to read and enjoy Jean Rhys's novel *Wide Sargasso Sea* (1966) without further knowledge of its writing and production history. However, if you also know that Rhys's novel builds on an earlier novel – Charlotte Brontë's *Jane Eyre* (1847) – in effect, critically responding to, or 'writing back' to, Brontë's novel, your understanding and appreciation of Rhys's novel is enhanced.

Concepts

As in other IB courses you will study, and like the 'areas of exploration', concepts work as an organising tool for your study of language and literature. Seven concepts inform the structure and organisation of this course. These are:

- identity
- culture
- creativity
- communication
- perspective
- transformation
- representation.

The concepts interact with the areas of exploration. At different times, the concepts will 'run through' the areas of exploration, providing a further tool with which to think about your study of literary works and non-literary texts. Like the areas of exploration, concepts are not directly assessed. Again, however, you should regard concepts as powerful cognitive tools to enhance your understanding of works and texts.

Concepts are an aspect of other IB courses, and working with concepts will therefore help you make interdisciplinary connections between the English A: Language and Literature course and other IB subjects, studies in the IB core and the wider world. How you work with concepts will depend on your teacher and your school. Some teachers will choose to use the concepts to construct enquiry-type questions, to help scaffold your study.

Theory of knowledge (TOK)

At different times during the English A: Language and Literature course, you, your teacher, or your fellow students will make, or be encouraged to make, connections to TOK. It may be tempting to see such connections as interesting but nothing to do with assessment. However, the opposite is true: TOK helps you develop skills of critical and lateral thinking. This is not *explicitly* measured in the assessment criteria. However, it is measured *implicitly*. Students who demonstrate critical thinking will be rewarded for this in examinations. For example, in language and literature, this might be demonstrated by an ability to read a text from different perspectives.

As in other subjects, language and literature provides examples of more general concerns that are relevant to assessment in TOK.

Approaches to learning (ATL)

Schools and teachers will differ in how they promote and support the development of ATL skills. ATL skills include communication, self-management and research skills. The development of such skills is lifelong, and your ability to demonstrate these skills is important to citizenship and academic success. You will need to manage your time purposefully, and to express your ideas clearly, succinctly and in an appropriate academic register.

As you move through your course, it will be helpful to reflect on how you are managing your independent study, and how your different linguistic skills are developing. If, for example, you find it difficult to keep pace with your studies or you find it challenging to express your ideas in writing, you should consider why this is and, in discussion with your teacher, put in place a plan to make improvements.

Accountability

Teachers of English A: Language and Literature will offer you, to a greater or lesser extent, freedom to make choices. As discussed under the ATL heading above, one important choice you must make is how you manage your studies and time. A further aspect of this is *academic honesty*. This includes a range of things. For example, your teacher will alert you if the course does not allow you to use the same literary work in two assessment components. Also, academic honesty means that you must produce your own independent work, and that you must not plagiarise by claiming that the work of others is your own.

Issues around academic honesty can sometimes seem scary, but they need not be. If you work with honest intent and consult your teacher where you are in doubt, issues around academic honesty are nothing to be afraid of.

Syllabus aims and assessment objectives

Syllabus aims

As a student, there is no requirement for you to have a detailed understanding of the course aims for English A: Language and Literature. However, having a broad sense of the aims of the course can help you understand, and put into context, what you are learning and why you are learning it.

The course has eight aims. You will:

1   study a wide range of literary works, non-literary texts and other media (e.g. moving film, audio, visual texts, etc.), which will come from a variety of times, places and cultures

2   develop productive and receptive skills, including writing, reading, speaking, listening, viewing, presenting and performing

3   develop skills that enable you to analyse and critically evaluate a wide range of text types

4   develop an understanding of the formal and aesthetic qualities of texts, showing appreciation of how they may be understood in a variety of ways

5   develop an understanding of texts and their relationship to cultural contexts, and local and global issues

6   develop an understanding of the relationship between language and literature and the other academic disciplines you are studying

7   develop an ability to collaborate confidently and creatively with others

8   develop an interest in and enjoyment of language and literature that you will carry over the course of your life.

Assessment objectives

As with the course aims, it is not expected that you will have a detailed knowledge of the assessment objectives. However, the better you understand what you will be assessed on, and why and how you will be assessed, the higher your chances of success in your examinations.

The examinations that you will take are informed by key assessment objectives, and these objectives form the basis for the marking criteria in all assessment components. There are three assessment objectives:

1 Knowledge, understanding and interpretation

In working with a range of texts, this objective requires you to demonstrate an understanding of:

- how meaning is produced and received
- the ways in which context influences how meaning is produced and received.

2 Analysis and evaluation

In working with a range of texts, this objective involves an ability to demonstrate how language and style contribute to meaning. You will critically engage with texts to show an appreciation of the relationships within and between texts. This objective also requires you to show how language and literature comment more broadly on human concerns.

3 Communication

This objective is about how you express your ideas. Most often, communication will be in formal academic contexts, and involve an ability to express your ideas clearly, accurately and appropriately in both speaking and writing.

Course assessment at a glance

You may not be looking forward to your examinations, but they are an important part of your learning. They provide an opportunity to show your knowledge and understanding, and to demonstrate your skills. Examinations encourage you to perform in specific conditions and under time constraints, and to channel your nervous energy. This challenge will help you to understand your English A: Language and Literature course much more than you would without the exams!

Remember that examinations are not intended to reveal what you do *not* know. On the contrary, examinations are an opportunity to show how far you have come, in knowledge, understanding and skills development, during your course of study.

Given the importance of examinations, it is essential to know what you will be assessed on, when and how.

Types of assessment

There are two types of assessment identified by the IB, which your teacher may sometimes refer to.

Formative assessment

This form of assessment is not directly used by the IB in examinations. Rather, it is a type of assessment that will be used by your teacher and, sometimes, by other students. It involves the assessment of your day-to-day learning, and is intended to help develop your understanding and skills over time. It may include a range of tasks that you submit for your learner portfolio. Formative assessment provides guidance to help you and your teacher identify your strengths and weaknesses, and helps you to consider and plan for improvement over your two-year course of study.

You cannot 'skip' formative assessment. It is an essential part of learning, and it prepares you for your examinations.

Summative assessment

As the name suggests, summative assessment is an 'end point' in your learning. It includes all the examinations that measure what you have learnt during your course. In your English A: Language and Literature course, this measurement involves the setting of marks using marking criteria, and these marks are translated into a final grade.

Internal and external assessment

There are two other forms of assessment that you will probably hear your teacher refer to frequently: *internal* assessment and *external* assessment.

All formative assessment is an example of internal assessment. This means that, mainly, your teacher assesses your work. Depending on the nature of the task, your teacher may not always mark your work using IB marking criteria. They may, for example, provide written and/or oral comments on your work, indicating your strengths and weaknesses, and providing advice for improvement.

Summative assessment, by contrast, may be either externally or internally assessed. Examinations that are externally assessed are submitted to IB examiners – often practising teachers in other schools – who use the IB's marking criteria to assess your work. Examinations that are internally assessed are marked by your own teacher using the IB's marking criteria. A sample of work from your class for this internal assessment is then submitted to an external IB moderator. The IB moderator is an examiner who provides a form of quality control, ensuring that your teacher is using the marking criteria fairly and correctly.

It is helpful for you to know whether an examination is externally or internally assessed. However, it makes no difference to how you are assessed, and both examiners (for external assessment) and moderators (for internal assessment) mark and moderate examinations anonymously using the IB's marking criteria. In other words, examiners and moderators do not know who you are or which school you attend, and you are always assessed only on the quality of your work.

For the purpose of the English A: Language and Literature course, only the individual oral is internally assessed. All other examinations, including Paper 1, Paper 2 and the higher-level essay, are externally assessed.

The following tables provide an overview of the summative examinations, what is involved in each of the examinations, and the relative weighting for each examined component. Remember to read the table that is relevant to you: they are slightly different for standard-level (SL) and higher-level (HL) students.

Assessment outline – for first examinations in 2021

Standard level

Assessment component	Weighting
External assessment: 3 hours in total	**70%**
Paper 1: Guided textual analysis **Time: 1 hour 15 minutes** **Total marks: 20** In this paper you will have two non-literary passages. Each passage will be of a different text type, and each passage will have one guiding question. You should choose *one* of the passages and write an analysis of it.	**35%**
Paper 2: Comparative essay **Time: 1 hour 45 minutes** **Total marks: 30** In this paper you will be given four general questions. You select *one* question to answer. In response to the question you choose, you should write about two literary works you have studied.	**35%**
Internal assessment **Individual oral** **Time: 15 minutes** **Total marks: 40** In this examination you will select an extract from one non-literary text and one literary work you have studied during your course. Having prepared for the examination in advance, you will discuss both extracts for 10 minutes. During this time, you should consider how a global issue of your choice is presented through the content and form. After your initial presentation, your teacher will spend 5 minutes asking you follow-up questions. Your presentation of ideas is always guided by this prompt: Examine the ways in which the global issue of your choice is presented through the content and form of one of the works and one of the texts that you have studied.	*30%*

Higher level

Assessment component	Weighting
External assessment: 4 hours in total plus the HL essay	**80%**
Paper 1: Guided textual analysis	**35%**
Time: 2 hours 15 minutes	
Total marks: 20	
In this paper you will have two non-literary passages. Each passage will be of a different text type, and each passage will have one guiding question. You should write an analysis of *both* of the passages.	
Paper 2: Comparative essay	**25%**
Time: 1 hour 45 minutes	
Total marks: 30	
In this paper you will be given four general questions. You select *one* question to answer. In response to the question you choose, you should write about two literary works you have studied.	
Higher-level (HL) essay	**20%**
Total marks: 20	
You will write an academic essay of between 1200 and 1500 words. You should, in discussion with your teacher, choose the focus of the essay yourself. The essay can be based on one non-literary text or on a collection of non-literary texts by the same author or on a literary work. Whether your focus is non-literary or literary, you should write about texts or works studied as part of your course.	
Internal assessment	
Individual oral	**20%**
Time: 15 minutes	
Total marks: 40	
In this examination you will select an extract from one non-literary text and one literary work you have studied during your course. Having prepared for the examination in advance, you will discuss both extracts for 10 minutes. During this time, you should consider how a global issue of your choice is presented through the content and form. After your initial presentation, your teacher will spend 5 minutes asking you follow-up questions.	
Your presentation of ideas is always guided by this prompt: Examine the ways in which the global issue of your choice is presented through the content and form of one of the works and one of the texts that you have studied.	

What are the differences between assessment at SL and HL?

Paper 1 is identical for SL and HL students. However, SL students choose and write analytically about *one* text, whereas HL students must write analytically about *both* texts. HL students, in other words, have no choice, whereas SL students do.

Paper 2 and the individual oral are identical for both HL and SL students. Only HL students are required to write the higher-level essay. There are differences in time limits and weighting between HL and SL. Where HL and SL students do the same examination with the same marking criteria, they are marked in exactly the same way. It is *not* the case that 'more is expected' of HL students.

What is the difference between 'seen' and 'unseen' examinations?

All of your examinations, except the Paper 1 examination, are 'seen' examinations. That is, they are based on works and texts that you have studied as part of your course. Although Paper 1 is an 'unseen' examination, your course of study will have equipped you to write analytically about a wide range of non-literary texts.

You do not know in advance of the Paper 2 examination what four questions you will be asked, but you will have decided which literary works you will use for your response.

What is the relationship between examinations and the selection of works and texts?

There is more about text selection a little later in this Introduction.

You should remember that examinations do not permit 'double-dipping'. This means, for example, that if your individual oral comes before your higher-level essay, you may not write about the same work or text in your higher-level essay that you discussed in your individual oral. Similarly, you may not write about the same literary works in your Paper 2 examination that you have already used in either the individual oral or the higher-level essay.

It is an important matter of academic honesty that you follow these rules when selecting your texts.

When will you take your examinations?

Paper 1 and 2 examinations always occur at the end of your second year of study. If you attend a school that is registered for *northern hemisphere* examinations, your Paper 1 and 2 examinations take place in May of your final year of study. If you study in a school that is registered for *southern hemisphere* examinations, your Paper 1 and 2 examinations take place in the November of your final year of study. If you are uncertain whether your school is registered for May or November examinations, you should check with your teacher or IB coordinator.

In the case of the individual oral and the higher-level essay, it is left to individual teachers and schools to decide when these will take place. Both assessments come at the end point of a process of teaching and learning. However, it is unlikely that either the individual oral or the higher-level essay will take place or be submitted before the end of your first year of study.

The individual oral

The individual oral (IO) is an assessment task that may feel rather daunting. It is spoken rather than written, and it may be one of the first IB examinations that you take. However, being a little nervous may help you focus and do well in the examination. The IO is an examination that you can prepare and practise for in advance. Section 4 of this book provides you with help and support on how to perform well in the IO, but here is an outline of what to expect in the examination.

In the IO you will always be asked to respond to this prompt:

Examine the ways in which the global issue of your choice is presented through the content and form of one of the works and one of the texts that you have studied.

Preparing for the IO

You have the freedom, in discussion with your teacher, to choose the global issue, and select literary and non-literary extracts of your own choice, before the examination.

Your teacher will tell you in advance where and when the IO will take place. You will not complete the IO until you have studied a number of literary works and non-literary texts. It is unlikely, therefore, that the IO will take place before the end of the first year of your course. It is important that you only select extracts from works and texts that you have studied.

Your IO will be recorded, and your teacher will be your examiner. Depending on your school's policy, your teacher may or may not tell you the mark you receive. Samples of your school's IO responses are submitted to the IB for moderation. It is possible, therefore, that the mark your teacher awards you will not be the final mark you receive.

Before your IO, you will receive a form from your teacher. This form, called an *outline*, allows you to list a maximum of ten bullet points. Each bullet point in your outline should be something you intend to discuss during your IO. Not later than one week before your IO, you must submit both the outline and your two chosen extracts – one literary, and the other non-literary – to your teacher.

What happens in the IO?

In the IO, you will bring the outline and your two extracts into the examination room. You must *not* annotate your outline or your extracts, and you must *not* simply read from your outline. Instead, the outline should prompt what you say. The examination tests your ability to speak, not your ability to read.

During the IO, you are required to speak for 10 minutes. Roughly, you should divide this time between both extracts. Remembering the guiding prompt: you should connect both of your extracts to the global issue of your choice, showing how it is presented. In addition, you need to connect your extracts to their wider body of work (for more about 'bodies of work' see the subsection on 'Selecting literary works and non-literary texts: what you need to know', in this Introduction).

After you have spoken for 10 minutes, your teacher will ask you questions. These questions are intended, as far as possible, to enhance your examination performance. For example, your teacher will ask you to extend your discussion, clarify points you have made and discuss points you may have omitted. Your teacher is not trying to 'catch you out'. Instead, your teacher will try to give you an opportunity to improve your overall IO mark.

It is important that you are, at all times, academically honest. This means, for example, that you develop ideas that are your own, and organise and structure your ideas independently. As you work towards your IO, you will receive advice and guidance from your teacher. Your teacher will not, however, give you explicit advice, and you should not expect this.

The learner portfolio

The learner portfolio is a compulsory course requirement. Your teacher will introduce it early in the course and you will return to it frequently throughout your study. The learner portfolio is not assessed by the IB. It is possible that your teacher or school will assess it. Where this happens, the assessment is for internal school purposes, not for the IB.

Your learner portfolio is not intended to be a collection of your 'best work'. Rather, it is a 'learning space' where all or much of your coursework is contained. It is expected that your knowledge, understanding and skills will develop over time. The portfolio is a tool that guides this development.

How to use your learner portfolio effectively

Using your learner portfolio diligently and consistently throughout your course is important, and doing so will help improve your skills. In your learner portfolio you will:

- include a range of entries
- be encouraged to reflect on your reading of literary works and non-literary texts
- make connections between different components of your course; between your course, TOK and CAS (creativity, activity and service); and between your course, other IB courses and the wider world – which enhances your learning
- use the space to prepare for your assessments.

It is possible that your learner portfolio will be digital or a collection of printed documents, or both. Your teacher will discuss and determine with you how best to create your learner portfolio.

Remember, the learner portfolio is important. It is compulsory and, where you use it effectively, a very powerful tool to improve your understanding, knowledge and skills.

As you approach the end of your course, the learner portfolio will be an important part of your revision. When the course is finished, you will be able to look at your learner portfolio and see the evidence of just how far you have come and how much you have learnt during your studies.

What should you include in your learner portfolio?

What you will include in your learner portfolio will depend, to a large extent, on you and your teacher. However, it is mandatory that you use your portfolio to clearly establish a link between what you have studied and the different assessment components. In part, this is to ensure compliance with course prescriptions and issues of academic honesty. For example, once you have 'used' a literary work for your individual oral, you may not return and 'reuse' that work in your HL essay (for HL students only) or Paper 2. On the one hand, the learner portfolio reminds you of what you have and have not studied; it helps you organise and navigate the course. On the other hand, where academic malpractice is suspected, the IB may ask to see a student's learner portfolio. If you are unclear about which literary works and non-literary texts you may refer to in your examinations, ask your teacher for advice.

Beyond this compulsory aspect of learner portfolios, it is up to students and teachers to decide what to include. For example:

- For the purpose of *self-management*, you may include visual maps that create links between literary works and non-literary texts studied, and between literary works, texts, concepts, global issues and other key ideas. Or, you may decide to create a glossary of key terms.
- It is important that you can *think critically and independently*. To develop these skills you need to, for example, respond frequently to the literary works and non-literary texts you study. This

may involve creating a study log or responding to questions from your teacher. You will almost certainly want to annotate, and write critical commentaries on, the literary works and non-literary texts you study.

- *Reflecting* on what you and others have written, read and said is very important. Reflection provides an opportunity to evaluate your progress and to identify areas where you could improve. There is an obvious connection among reflection and self-assessment, developing self-awareness, and examination success.

- At various times in your course, your teacher may ask you to engage in *creative tasks* to include in your learner portfolio. There is a correlation between affective engagement and success. That is, if you immerse yourself in an activity you enjoy, you are more likely to do it well. Suppose your teacher asks you to create an advertisement. The act of doing so forces you to think about what formal features and linguistic structures typically constitute an advertisement. This kind of focused thinking is important. If, for example, an advertisement or a different type of persuasive text should appear in a Paper 1 examination, the work you previously did in creating your own advertisement will be very valuable. Therefore, when your teacher asks you to do creative tasks, do not dismiss them as a waste of time. Instead, enjoy the opportunity to build the creative skills required for success in your course.

Selecting literary works and non-literary texts: what you need to know

How will you choose which literary works and texts you will study?

The English A: Language and Literature course is guided by important principles of *choice* and *autonomy*. This means that for you as a student, there will be opportunities to make your own choices of which literary works and non-literary texts you study, and which works and texts you focus on in your examinations.

However, the degree of choice and freedom you actually have will vary, depending on the school you attend. Teachers in all schools must work within a range of IB guidelines. As a student, you do not need to know exactly what these are, but it does mean that schools, teachers and students *cannot* study and read whatever they like. Also, schools may have different budgets for purchasing books, and teachers may have their own preferences. These practical considerations may also impact on your choice and autonomy.

During the course you will study literary works such as novels, plays and poems. You will also study non-literary texts such as advertisements, news stories and blogs. Sometimes, you will study non-literary texts as *bodies of work* – for example, *several* news stories by the same journalist. At other times you will study non-literary texts independently and discretely – for example, one news story. You should make sure that you understand which is which – a body of work or a discrete individual text – because some assessment components require you to discuss the body of work and others do not.

This table identifies whether each assessment component assesses knowledge and understanding of literary works, non-literary texts or both, and whether or not the idea of a body of work is relevant to that assessment component.

Assessment component	Assesses knowledge and understanding of literary works, non-literary texts or both?	Where knowledge and understanding of non-literary texts is assessed, is the notion of 'bodies of work' relevant?
Paper 1	Non-literary	No
Paper 2	Literary	Not relevant
Individual oral	Both	Yes
Higher-level essay	Either/or	Yes, if you choose to focus on non-literary texts

If you are uncertain about the idea of a 'body of work', you should ask your teacher for further guidance. This has implications for assessment and your autonomy to make choices.

How is your choice limited?

Your teacher will tell you, and introduce you to, the literary works and non-literary texts (including bodies of work) you will study, at the appropriate point in your course. They may or may not offer you a choice. You will, of course, read literary works and texts sequentially – you cannot read everything at once! Paper 1 will precede Paper 2, and both examinations take place at the end of your course. The IO and the higher-level essay (for HL students only) both take place before Papers 1 and 2, and your teacher will decide in which order and when.

It is likely that both your IO and your higher-level essay will take place *before* you have read all of your literary works and texts. You can therefore choose to focus only on the literary works and non-literary texts you have studied *before* these examinations.

In a two-year course, HL students study *six* literary works and SL students study *four*. Both HL and SL students study a wide range of non-literary texts, some of which are studied as 'bodies of work'. If, for example, your teacher schedules the IO at the end of your first year of study, your choice of works and texts is limited to those you have studied *up to that point*. If you have studied just two literary works, then that is your choice. Even though your choice may be limited to just two literary works, it is important that *you* make the choice. You are strongly advised to seek your teacher's advice and to discuss your decision, but your teacher *cannot* make this choice for you.

By the end of the course, you will have studied all of your literary works and non-literary texts. You must *not* reuse a literary work or non-literary text in one examination component that you previously used in a different examination component. For example, if, as an HL student, the first literary work you study is Shakespeare's *Hamlet*, and in discussion with your teacher you decide to discuss an extract from the play in your IO, this is absolutely fine. However, you must not then write about *Hamlet* in either your HL essay or Paper 2. This kind of 'double-dipping' is not allowed, and is a limitation on your choice of literary works and texts.

As you can see, you will have some freedom to choose, but there are important limitations on your choice. You should select literary works and non-literary texts that you have enjoyed studying and that you think will provide good material for your examinations.

Selecting literary works: what teachers need to know

In the previous subsection, you found out what you need to know about selecting literary works. It can also be useful for you to understand what teachers need to know when selecting literary works for you to study in your course. An outline of the most important points is given here.

Standard level

Standard-level (SL) students must study at least *four* literary works, of which:

- at least *one* must be a work originally written in English by an author on the Prescribed Reading List (an IB publication that lists authors across languages)

- at least *one* must be a work originally in translation (i.e. not originally in English) by an author on the Prescribed Reading List

- *two* works may be chosen freely and may be in translation.

There must be at least *one* work for each of the three areas of exploration (see the 'Syllabus overview' earlier in this Introduction). Works studied must include at least *two* literary forms, *two* periods, *two* places (all of which are defined by the Prescribed Reading List) and cover at least *two* continents.

Higher level

Higher-level (HL) students must study at least *six* literary works, of which:

- at least *two* must be works originally written in English by authors on the Prescribed Reading List

- at least *two* must be works originally in translation (i.e. not originally in English) by authors on the Prescribed Reading List

- *two* works may be chosen freely and may be in translation.

There must be at least *two* works for each area of exploration. Works studied must include at least *three* literary forms, *three* periods, *three* places (all of which are defined by the Prescribed Reading List) and cover at least *two* continents.

Command terms

The IB uses a range of command terms across all subject areas. Command terms are the key words that are used in the construction of questions and prompts. For example, in the following prompt, the command term is *discuss*:

Discuss the ways in which the writer constructs a persuasive argument in this text.

Where command terms are used, their meaning is unchanging, and it is very useful to have a clear sense of what command terms mean. The reason for this is simple: if in an examination you do *not* understand the question or do *not* respond to the question, you will do much less well than if you directly address the question, showing an obvious awareness of command terms.

Command terms are relevant to *all* of the assessment components for English A: Language and Literature. In the IO, the question/prompt is unchanging. In Paper 1, you are required to construct a focused response and it is likely that this focus will come from the guiding question that accompanies each text extract. In Paper 2, you must respond to one of four questions, and each question may begin with a different command term. You could argue that the higher-level essay has no questions or prompts, and thus command terms are irrelevant. However, this is not entirely the case. That is, the higher-level essay ought to be enquiry-based, and enquiry often involves establishing a question of your own choosing that, in turn, you aim to respond to.

Here is a list of the command terms that are the most relevant to the study of language and literature:

Analyse: Break down in order to show the most essential elements, parts or structure.

Comment: Make a considered judgement about something based on available evidence.

Compare: Consider the similarities between two or more things.

Contrast: Consider the differences between two or more things.

Discuss: Present a considered and balanced argument. Include a range of arguments and perspectives. Synthesise arguments, bringing together different perspectives and using evidence to support claims.

Evaluate: Make an assessment of something, considering a range of strengths and limitations.

Examine: Consider an argument, looking at underlying assumptions and the relationships between claims made.

Explain: Give a full account of something, including reasons, causes and outcomes.

To what extent: Consider the strengths and limitations of arguments or claims.

Paper 1: Guided textual analysis (SL/HL)

In this section you will:

- learn about the requirements of Paper 1: Guided textual analysis and how it is assessed
- develop and practise the skills needed to succeed in this paper
- assess examples of responses to guided textual analysis questions, and develop your critical awareness about what the examination requires of you.

> **Learning objectives**
>
> - Gain a better understanding of the types of question you can expect in your Paper 1 examination.
> - Develop strategies to improve your writing about non-literary texts.
> - Learn about the conventions of the non-literary text types you could write about in Paper 1.

Getting started

The term 'text' can be interpreted in different ways. All texts convey meaning, but during your course you will be expected to develop an understanding of both literary and non-literary texts.

Literary texts can include: poems, short stories, prose, non-fiction, novels, plays.

Non-literary texts can include: advertisements, brochures, speeches, websites, photographs, information booklets, film posters, travel writing, song lyrics.

Both literary and non-literary texts have conventions which shape them and inform our reading of them. Understanding how and why they were crafted, and being able to write informed analyses, is central to making sustained progress towards all the assessments.

In this chapter you will explore the following text types:

Number	Title	Author/source	Text type
1	From *Salt, Fat, Acid, Heat*	Samin Nosrat	Cookbook
2	'Anatomy of a perfect grilled cheese sandwich'	Wendy MacNaughton	Illustration
3	The Set Text	Tom Gauld	Cartoon
4	From *In Cold Blood*	Truman Capote	Non-fiction/novel
5	'Wealthy Farmer, 3 Of Family Slain	*New York Times*	News feature
6	'Your Army Needs You'	British Army/ Capita	Advertisement campaign
7	'Beautifully Obvious'	WeTransfer/ WeAreCognitive	Animated advertisement
8	From *Beneath the Roses*	Gregory Crewdson	Photograph
9	'Why Wikipedia is so great'	Wikipedia editors	Webpage
10	'To my old master'	Jourdon Anderson	Personal letter

Start by asking yourself the following questions, and making notes of your answers in your portfolio:

- Which non-literary works have you read so far?

- Which non-fiction text types have you enjoyed the most? Why? You may want to think about:
  - the subject matter
  - the writer's style, including any uses of humour
  - the use of evidence.

- What similarities and differences have you noticed between these text types?

- Which non-fiction text types have you enjoyed the *least*? You may want to think about:
  - the subject matter
  - any political bias in the text which you disagree with
  - the writer's style, including emotive language
  - the lack of evidence.

- What similarities and differences are there between these text types?

The range of text types you may be asked to write about is very wide. You could be asked to comment on a complete piece of writing, or an extract. The best preparation for Paper 1 is simply to read as many non-literary texts as possible. However, you should go beyond that and think *critically* about the texts you are analysing, and about what is shaping your understanding. Every time you read a new text you should consciously consider the *author*, the *text* and the *reader*.

TIP

Every text you encounter – whether it is an advertisement for clothes, a tweet, a Facebook post, a flyer for an event, or a film review – is an opportunity to improve yourself as a critical reader. For each non-fiction text you encounter, ask yourself two basic questions: Is this text effective? Why?

The author of a non-fiction text could be anonymous, or could even be a group of people (for example, an advertising company responsible for a particular image or campaign, such as those later in this section, used to promote the British Army and WeTransfer). The reader is – of course – you, but you may not have been part of the original intended audience, and so you should have an awareness of other readers. This will prompt you to ask questions about the *context* of the text: When was it written? Who was it intended for? Has it changed over time?

TIP

Remember to use your learner portfolio to write down your responses to these questions. This can help you reflect on areas that need further work, but also allow you to track the progress you are making.

ACTIVITY

Look at the following list of text types. List as many conventions as you can for each text type, which shape how they are written.

- advertisements
- autobiographies
- biographies
- blogs
- diaries
- essays
- information booklets
- instruction manuals
- letters
- magazine articles
- newspaper reports
- social media posts

Consider the following questions:

1 How are these texts similar?

2 How are they different?

You might think about audience and purpose, but remember to write down your thoughts, as these may be helpful for the tasks later in this section.

Now answer these questions:

1 Which of these text types are the most 'literary' in style?

2 Which are the most 'non-literary' in style?

ACTIVITY

How do you explain your answers to these last two questions? Where possible, find examples to support your points.

Think about other text types. Which of the following have you explored and which are still unfamiliar to you?

- comic strips
- political cartoons
- posters
- photographs
- speeches

Which of these text types would you be confident to write about in Paper 1, and which would you feel less certain about? Answering this question will help you focus on what types of text to read as you prepare for the examination.

Outline of assessment and task

Both SL and HL students take the same Paper 1. This paper is worth 35% of your final grade in English A: Language and Literature. Here are the key features of Paper 1.

For SL

- You will take this paper at the end of your course.
- You are allowed 1 hour 15 minutes for this exam.
- You have to choose *one* non-literary text from *two* different text types.
- Each text has an accompanying 'guiding question', which will focus on a technical or formal aspect of the passage.
- You do not have to address the guiding question directly, but you should write an analysis of a particular aspect of the passage.
- You will not be allowed to take any texts with you into the exam.

For HL

- You will take this paper at the end of your course.
- You are allowed 2 hours 15 minutes for this exam.
- You will be asked to write on *both* non-literary texts from two different text types.
- Each text has an accompanying 'guiding question', which will focus on a technical or formal aspect of the passage.
- You do not have to address the guiding question, but you should provide an analysis of a particular aspect of the passage.
- You will not be allowed to take any texts with you into the exam.

For both SL and HL, there are four assessment criteria for Paper 1.

Criterion A	Understanding and interpretation	5 marks
Criterion B	Analysis and evaluation	5 marks
Criterion C	Focus and organisation	5 marks
Criterion D	Language	5 marks
Total		20 marks

Each of these criteria has grade descriptors to help students, teachers and examiners evaluate the quality of completed work. You should familarise yourself with the criteria and level descriptors so that you understand how you are being assessed, and how you may need to improve your work in order to move up to a higher grade band.

Here are the four criteria with the key words and phrases for each grade.

Criterion A: Understanding and interpretation

Marks	Level descriptor
0	Does not reach the standard required.
1	**Little** understanding of the literal meaning of the text, with little appropriate evidence.
2	**Some** understanding of the literal meaning of the text, with some appropriate evidence.
3	**Satisfactory** interpretation of some aspects of the text. References generally relevant.
4	**Thorough** understanding of the literal meaning of the text. References to the text are relevant.
5	**Thorough and perceptive** understanding of the text. References to the text are well chosen.

Criterion B: Analysis and evaluation

Marks	Level descriptor
0	Does not reach the standard required.
1	The response is **descriptive** and does not analyse textual features.
2	**Some appropriate** analysis, but mostly descriptive.
3	**Generally appropriate** analysis.
4	Some **insightful analysis**. Good evaluation of textual features.
5	**Insightful and convincing** analysis. Very good evaluation of textual features.

Criterion C: Focus and organisation

Marks	Level descriptor
0	Does not reach the standard required.
1	**Little** organisation.
2	**Some** organisation.
3	**Adequately** organised.
4	**Well** organised.
5	**Effectively** organised.

Criterion D: Language

Marks	Level descriptor
0	Does not reach the standard required.
1	Language is **rarely** clear, with a lot of errors in vocabulary and grammar.
2	Language is **sometimes** clear, with some errors and inconsistencies in vocabulary and grammar.
3	Language is clear, with an **adequate** level of accuracy in vocabulary and grammar.
4	Language is clear, with a **good** level of accuracy in vocabulary and grammar.
5	Language is very clear, with a **high** level of accuracy in vocabulary and grammar.

Self and peer-assessment

Reflect on each of these criteria, and consider the strengths and weaknesses in your own work. Which areas could you focus on in order to improve?

- How would you grade the last piece of writing you did, if you applied these criteria?
- Swap a recent piece of work with a partner and give them a mark out of 20 using these criteria. Can you support your mark with evidence from the text?
- Do you agree with the mark applied to your own work? How could you improve it, using the criteria and level descriptors?

How to approach guided textual analysis questions

The range of possible texts you could be asked to write on in Paper 1 is almost limitless. That could be intimidating – or it could be liberating! Unlike Paper 2, you cannot 'revise' for Paper 1 by learning lots of quotations: there are none to learn. What you can do, however, is think about the sorts of questions you might be asked, and become familiar with the features and conventions of different text types. Familiarity with the assessment criteria will help you focus on *how* to answer any questions you could be asked.

The questions themselves have to be very broad in order to allow students with very different backgrounds to access them. As with Paper 2, in Paper 1 – at both SL and HL – patterns begin to emerge, with questions focusing on how language 'entertains' or 'interests' the reader. Visual texts may include references to layout, fonts and other design features.

Every question will ask you how *effective* the texts are. In order for you to answer this successfully, you will need to develop your skills in evaluating language, both written and visual.

Analysing a text

Success in Paper 1 depends on knowing how to analyse a text, and how to write an effective analysis. Understanding the author's intentions is key, and for this you will need to develop the skills that will enable you to identify subtle and nuanced ideas. In literary texts, these elements can be conveyed using things like irony, humour, satire and pastiche, and in non-literary texts, they can be made visual through the use of images. You should also learn to be aware of the possible alternative readings of a text, so that your analysis is wide-ranging, balanced and sophisticated.

For Criterion A (Understanding and interpretation), you will have to demonstrate not only that you understand the literal meaning of the text but also its 'larger implications' and its 'subtleties'. You will have to show, in your analysis, how language shapes meaning, and the guiding question that accompanies each text will help you think about this.

Exam-style question for Paper 1

Read the following passage (Text A) from *Salt, Fat, Acid, Heat* by the American-Iranian writer and chef Samin Nosrat. An HL student, Serene, has added her annotations to the text. The numbers correspond to her annotations, which are given later.

> **ACTIVITY**
>
> *Salt, Fat, Acid, Heat* is a highly successful cookbook and Netflix series. As you read the extract, think about Nosrat's writing style, as well as what she wants to convey.

Text A

What is heat?

Heat is the element of transformation.[1] No matter its source, heat triggers the changes that take our food from raw to cooked, runny to set, flabby to firm, flat to risen, and pale to golden brown.[2]

Unlike Salt, Fat, and Acid, Heat is flavourless and intangible. But its effects are quantifiable. Heat's sensory cues,[3] including sizzles, spatters, crackles, steam, bubbles, aromas, and browning,[4] are often more important than a thermometer. All of your senses – including common sense[5] – will help you gauge heat's effects on food.

Exposure to heat changes foods in many different, but predictable, ways. Once familiar with how different foods respond to heat, you'll make better choices about how to shop at the market, plan a menu, and cook every dish.[6] Turn your attention away from the oven dial or the knob of the stove and towards the food you're cooking. Heed the clues: is the food browning, firming, shrinking, crisping, burning, falling apart, swelling, or cooking unevenly?[7]

These cues matter considerably more than whether you're cooking on an electric rather than gas stove, on a makeshift camping grill rather than a grand marble hearth, or whether your oven is set to 180°C or 190°C.[8]

Just as I learned from watching cooks all around the world, no matter what you're cooking, or what heat sources you're using, the aim is always the same: apply heat at the right level, and at the right rate, so that the surface of a food and its interior are done cooking at the same time.[9]

Think about making a grilled cheese sandwich.[10] The goal is to use the right level of heat so that the bread turns golden-brown-toasty-delicious[11] at the same time that the cheese melts. Heat it too quickly and you'll burn the outside and be left with the undercooked centre – burnt bread, unmelted cheese. Heat it too slowly, and you'll dry the whole thing out before the surface has a chance to brown.

View everything you cook like that grilled cheese sandwich:[12] is the skin of the roast chicken golden brown by the time the bird is cooked? Is the asparagus cooked all the way through by the time it's developed the perfect char from the grill? Is the lamb chop evenly browned, all of its fat rendered by the time the meat is perfectly medium-rare?[13]

Just as with Salt, Fat, and Acid, the first step to getting the results you want from Heat is to know what you're after. Know about your goals in the kitchen in terms of flavours and textures. Do you want your food to be browned? Crisp? Tender? Soft? Chewy? Caramelised? Flaky? Moist?[14]

Next, work backward. Make a clear plan for yourself using sensory landmarks[15] to guide your goal. For example, if you want to end up with a bowl of flavourful, snowy white mashed potatoes, then think about the last step: mashing potatoes with butter and sour cream, and tasting and

TIP

Guiding questions

Remember, you do not have to respond directly to the guiding questions that accompany the texts on Paper 1. But they are there to help you structure your essay, and bring it into clearer focus. You can't write about *everything* in the examination, so think carefully about what aspect of the text the guiding question is asking you to explore.

adjusting for salt. To get there, you'll need to peel and cut the potatoes. There's your recipe.[16] For something more complicated – say, crispy pan-fried potatoes – you'll want to end with a golden-brown crust and tender interior. So the last step will be frying in hot fat to achieve crispiness. To get there, make sure the potatoes are tender inside – simmer them in salted water. To get there, peel and cut them. There's another recipe.

This is good cooking, and simpler than you might think.[17]

From *Salt, Fat, Acid, Heat* by Samin Nosrat

Guiding question:

In what ways does the language used in this text reflect its purpose?

Text B

Look at this visual text, which is an illustration from *Salt, Fat, Acid, Heat*. Consider the effect of the formal features that the illustrator, Wendy MacNaughton, has used.

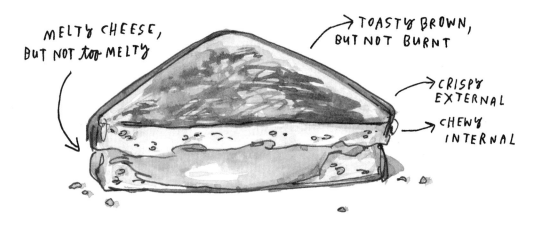

Guiding question:

How are formal features such as fonts and visuals used to create an effect in this illustration?

Planning an answer

When thinking about planning your analysis, the first steps are to read the guiding question and then begin to annotate the text.

Annotating the text is a key step in making sense of it. Write in pencil so that you can easily change any ideas if you change your mind later. Annotating a text may lead you to ask yourself a number of questions: this is fine, but then make sure you answer them in your analysis.

The same skills that you are developing when you annotate a literary work can be applied to a non-literary text. However, you should bear in mind that non-literary texts very often have different intentions and audiences: they can provide you with instructions on how to put together a desk, or persuade you to buy a new phone or computer. Remember to think carefully about the purpose of the texts you are writing about.

Analysing Text A

Here are Serene's annotations to Text A. The numbers correspond to the numbers in the text.

1   Why is this an effective opening sentence?

2   What is the effect of this list of words associated with the semantic field of cooking?

3   Why is 'sensory cues' a memorable phrase?

4   Again, Nosrat explores the semantics of cooking: is it effective the second time?

5   Common sense is not one of our senses: does its inclusion work here? What is the effect?

6   This is a bold claim to make about how the reader might improve as a cook: what purpose is behind it?

7   For the third time, Nosrat creates an impact by adding words connected with cooking: how successful is it?

8   Another big claim to make: is this the main purpose behind this text?

9   This whole paragraph is doing various things: the opening sentence creates a clear impression of the author, and the succeeding sentences go on to state something very obvious. To what extent does the paragraph work, and why (or why not)?

10   Why choose a grilled cheese sandwich to illustrate the point?

11   What is the effect of this compound adjective?

12   Is this hyperbole? Is it serious, or for effect?

13   A selection of foods is given here: why does she choose these? What does it say about her intended audience?

14   Another list of words associated with cooking: again, how effective is this? Is this technique over used?

15   Is the phrase 'sensory landmarks' effective? Or is it pretentious?

16   These bold, simple statements are a feature of the text: what purpose do they serve, and how successful are they?

17   Is this final sentence the essence of the text? Or has she shown – with the profusion of descriptive words – that cooking is actually a very complex process?

Self-assessment

Now have a go at writing the opening paragraphs of an analysis of Text A. Once you have done this, use the criteria to assess what you have written.

Then read the following opening paragraphs written by Serene, using her annotations to the text, and look at her teacher's comments and marks.

If you are unsure about how to grade your own opening paragraphs, use her teacher's assessment as a benchmark to assess your own.

Serene's opening paragraphs

The opening sentence in Nosrat's text is highly effective. She is clearly very aware of what her audience wants, not just in terms of getting a recipe for a toasted cheese sandwich (which most would probably know), but explaining the visceral appeal of cooking something so simple. The semantic field employed by the author is skilled at making something familiar – in this case heat – become truly transformational. The balance of a number of polarities – 'raw to cooked', 'runny to set', 'flabby to firm' not only convey the mutability of heat, but also how it changes the unappealing to the appealing. The language in the opening section makes no mention of the difficulties that cooking can create: for Nosrat each of the transformations are as smooth and painless as the move from 'flat to risen', or from 'pale to golden brown'.

The second paragraph is equally articulate, and repeats similar tropes, including a wide range of intensifiers associated with cooking. What is different here is Nosrat's use of vocabulary – an objective register ('quantifiable', 'thermometer', 'gauge') with an obvious pleasure in words that have an onomatopoeic effect, including 'sizzles, spatters, crackles' and 'bubbles'. Such words remind us that, although there is a science behind preparing food, there has to be pleasure too. Nosrat knows her audience well, and this skilful use of language exemplifies this. Hers is an educated audience that wants to be informed about food, but also appreciates the aesthetics behind it.

Here is how Serene's teacher applied the assessment criteria to these opening paragraphs.

Criterion A: Understanding and interpretation	There is a thorough and perceptive understanding of the meaning of the text, and an appreciation of its subtleties.	5 marks out of 5
Criterion B: Analysis and evaluation	This is convincing, and, as a limited analysis of the text's features, this shows a good evaluation of how language shapes meaning. It would have been good to see an acknowledgement of tone in these opening paragraphs. Clearly demonstrates an understanding of the author's purpose.	4 marks out of 5
Criterion C: Focus and organisation	This is well organised and coherent, with a focused analysis. The rather mechanical paragraphing – with each paragraph following the paragraphing of the original text – seems inflexible. A more fluent, holistic analysis would have supported her answer.	4 marks out of 5
Criterion D: Language	The language used is sophisticated and clear, with each word well chosen. A more focused technical language, even at this early stage, would have been successful.	4 marks out of 5
Total		**17 marks**

Peer-assessment

Discuss the opening paragraphs of Serene's essay, and her teacher's assessment, with a fellow student.

- Do you agree with the teacher's assessment of Serene's opening paragraphs?

- What parts of their assessment do you disagree with?

- Serene lost a mark in three of the criteria. Do you think this is justified? Why?

- Discussing differences between your assessment and the teacher's can help you understand where marks are awarded – and lost – for your own work.

Analysing Text B

For Text B, Serene made notes on the following features:

- the style of font used

- the overall 'amateur' appearance of the image

- the inclusion of the 'insertion' symbol between 'A' and 'Grilled'

- the informal language ('toasty', 'melty', 'chewy').

All of these are valid, but her teacher advised her that she was neglecting the bigger ideas in the text. She suggested to Serene that she include these interpretations in a wider analysis of Text B, which would include an evaluation of:

- purpose

- style and structure

- audience

- meaning.

Peer-assessment

Discuss with a partner how you would advise Serene to proceed with her analysis of Text B.

- How would you incorporate what she wants to explore with what her teacher advises her?

- How would you maximise marks in each of the assessment criteria?

Try planning this as a pair, or on your own. Spend 20 minutes on this before doing the next activity.

ACTIVITY

Write a 400-word analysis of Text B, which follows your agreed plan.

> **REFLECT**
>
> What aspect of Text B did you find most difficult to write about?
>
> Choose another non-literary text and write an analysis that focuses specifically on this aspect. For example, if you found it challenging to write about 'purpose', pick an advertisement, an information booklet or even another cookbook, and focus on that aspect.

TIP

Think about how *meaning* is constructed in all the text types you read, whether they are written or visual.

Peer-assessment

For the activity and the 'reflect' exercise, swap your work with a partner and provide feedback on each other's work, to show where marks might be gained and lost. Remember to be constructive and encouraging in your feedback.

Through practice and focus, you will improve in these key areas.

Remember to use your learner portfolio as you prepare for all your assessments.

For Paper 1, you could record impressions of texts you have read or seen in magazines, online, on television or even on advertising hoardings and billboards. You might focus on particular skills – such as analysing visual texts – and track how you have tried to improve in this area.

Try writing your own guiding questions and keep these in your learner portfolio, or share them with fellow students.

Analysing cartoons

Look at the following cartoon by British cartoonist Tom Gauld.

ACTIVITY

Practise trying to make sense of something you find funny: why does it work?

Why does something that is intended to amuse you fail to do so?

Explaining a joke usually results in making it unfunny, but thinking about why it works is an important part in developing as a skilled reader of texts. Consider the following questions.

- What was your first response when you read this cartoon? Did it resonate with you? Did it make you smile, or sad, or both?

- Is the point the cartoonist is making comic or something more serious?

- How would you describe the characterisation of the book here? Naive? Innocent? Is it deliberately working against how you would characterise a set text?

- Who is this cartoon aimed at? Teachers or students? Or a more general readership?

Look at some of the comments made about this cartoon:

- 'Heartbreaking'

- 'After seeing this it made me want to hug my books. Poor books.'

- 'Sadly, this is what happens when we dictate whole class "novel studies" and then require a text analysis.'

- 'That is so unbelievably sad that I am nearly in tears here.'

- 'It's wonderful! Funny and touching. You feel sorry for the set text.'

- 'So true it hurts RT.' [RT = retweet]

- 'How is this as emotionally charged as Schindler's List?'

- 'Sadly, books went this way AGES ago.'

- 'This cartoon is made of awesome.'

ACTIVITY

To what extent does the response of other readers change our perception of a text?

Are some responses more valid than others? Why?

Are all of these comments intended to be taken seriously?

TIP

Learning the key features of different text types takes time, but it is time well spent. Familiarise yourself with the following terms used to analyse cartoons and graphic novels, and apply them when you write your essay.

negative space	gutter
speech bubble	symbols
panel	punchline

Using and understanding the correct terminology will help you to meet the requirements of Criterion D. It will also help you evaluate and analyse the effectiveness of the text, to do well in Criterion B.

TIP

Writing about humour

Writing about something humorous, especially in an examination, can be challenging. Identifying something which is ironic, satirical or deliberately self-deprecating can present you with a difficult series of evaluations. How effective is it, and how serious a message is contained in something that might appear to be light-hearted? Humour can convey serious issues, but much of its subtlety can be lost if you don't share the same sense of humour.

Sample student response

Ahmad is an IB student in his first year of the diploma. Here is his first attempt at evaluating Gauld's cartoon, written under timed conditions.

First draft

Tom Gauld's cartoon strip is very funny. Its humour springs not just from what is written, but what is drawn. The 'action' takes place over five sections, and focuses on one character - the set text. The artwork is really simple: a book talks to the audience (us) about how excited he is to be the student's 'set text'. He then goes through a number of different relationships that he is looking forward to having with the student, ranging from a book that the student looks up on Wikipedia, to a book that has been made into a film. The final section reveals the truth: that the student has no intention of reading the book but would prefer instead to simply watch the film before writing the essay. This is funny because it reminds the student of behaviour he or she might have been guilty of, and it is from this guilt that the humour can be found.

Ahmad's teacher gave him some feedback on his analysis, and asked him to look at how he could improve it with reference to Criteria B (Analysis and evaluation) and D (Language). Here is Ahmad's second draft, in which he attempts to address these issues. The changes that he has made are highlighted, using a different colour for each of the two criteria.

ACTIVITY

Once you have read Ahmad's analysis, suggest how it could be rewritten and improved to better meet the requirements of Criteria B and D.

Second draft

Tom Gauld's cartoon is a sophisticated analysis of the often complex relationship a student can have with his or her 'set text'. Its humour springs not just from what is written, but also from what is drawn, and, like all effective comedy, it connects with us because it has a universal theme (in this case, guilt). Each panel cleverly articulates a different set of expectations by the central (and only) character in the cartoon - the Set Text. What does not change, however, is the optimism of the Set Text: the speech bubbles reveal a naïvity at odds with reality. In each panel the negative space remains mostly unshaded and neutral, and the facial expressions of the Set Text modulate only slightly: this drawing style is as childlike as the character it depicts. The language used is colloquial, with phrases used in conversational English, such as 'Hello there!', 'totally fine', 'Ah, I see'. And although this is constructed as a dialogue between the student and the Set Text, the conversation only goes one way as the student ignores the attention-seeking words used by the Set Text. Each panel has, effectively, the same punchline: namely, that the book's expectations are not met by the student, but that this does not stop him remaining hopeful that they're both going to have 'a great time'. The humour comes from the various elements used by Gauld to describe this relationship, and also from a recognition that all of us, at some time or another, are guilty of being that unseen student.

Colour coding:

Criterion B (Analysis and evaluation)

Criterion D (Language)

As you can see from the changes highlighted in his second draft, Ahmad's work has paid off. He has focused on developing both Criteria B and D, and has improved his answer in both areas.

ACTIVITY

Try writing **one** of the following:

- a *third draft* of Ahmad's essay, in which you develop Criteria A (Understanding and interpretation) and C (Focus and organisation).

- the *next two paragraphs* of Ahmad's analysis in which you try to equally address *each* of the four criteria.

Peer-assessment

Swap your work with a partner and award marks for each criterion. Make sure that you are able to support the marks you award with evidence from the level descriptors for each criterion, given earlier in this section.

REFLECT

Think about what you do when you are first introduced to a text.

- Do you read the blurb on the back?

- Do you look up the author online?

- How do you judge the text?

- Is it important to you whether you are already familiar with the author's work, or whether the text is well known or not?

- What other factors contribute to how you approach a text?

The importance of context

The more you read, the more you will understand. Reading creates connections, and connections open up ideas. Central to understanding the many different aspects of a text is the context in which it was first written and read:

Contexts of *production*: Who was it written by, and why? When was it written and published?
Contexts of *reception*: How was it received? How influential has it been? Has it dated, or not? Why?

Contexts are dynamic and always changing. Texts evolve through time, responding to different interpretations and shifting as social issues change. When analysing a text, you should focus on how themes can extend – not only through time but also across countries and cultures. This universality of human experience is at the centre of how we read, write and respond to literary and non-literary texts.

Criteria A focuses on 'Understanding and intepretation', and Criterion B focuses on 'Analysis and evaluation'. Your knowledge of context will help you to improve your performance in both criteria. It enables you to widen your understanding of the text, and demonstrate to the examiner that you are aware of why the author made certain choices.

Time and space

Through this area of exploration, you will see how context depends on the interconnection between the local and the global. It is also interesting to think about how a text's meaning and impact change over time.

How can awareness of context deepen your knowledge and understanding of a text?

Read the following passage. Do not search for it online, or try to find out anything about it. If you already know the text this passage was taken from, try to focus on the text itself, rather than the context in which it was written.

The village of Holcomb stands on the high wheat plains of western Kansas, a lonesome area that other Kansans call "out there." Some seventy miles east of the Colorado border, the countryside, with its hard blue skies and desert-clear air, has an atmosphere that is rather more Far West than Middle West. The local accent is barbed with a prairie twang, a ranch-hand nasalness, and the men, many of them, wear narrow frontier trousers, Stetsons, and high-heeled boots with pointed toes. The land is flat, and the views are awesomely extensive; horses, herds of cattle, a white cluster of grain elevators rising as gracefully as Greek temples are visible long before a traveler reaches them.

Holcomb, too, can be seen from great distances. Not that there is much to see—simply an aimless congregation of buildings divided in the center by the main-line tracks of the Santa Fe Railway, a haphazard hamlet bounded on the south by a brown stretch of the Arkansas (pronounced "Ar-kan-sas") River, on the north by a highway, Route 50, and on the east and west by prairie lands and wheat fields. After rain, or when snowfalls thaw, the streets, unnamed, unshaded, unpaved, turn from the thickest dust into the direst mud. At one end of the town stands a stark old stucco structure, the roof of which supports an electric sign—"dance"—but the dancing has ceased and the advertisement has been dark for several years. Nearby is another building with an irrelevant sign, this one in flaking gold on a dirty window— "Holcomb Bank." The bank failed in 1933, and its former counting rooms have been converted into apartments. It is one of the town's two "apartment houses," the second being a ramshackle mansion known, because a good part of the local school's faculty lives there, as the Teacherage. But the majority of Holcomb's homes are one-story frame affairs, with front porches.

Down by the depot, the postmistress, a gaunt woman who wears a rawhide jacket and denims and cowboy boots, presides over a falling-apart post office. The depot itself, with its peeling sulphur-colored paint, is equally melancholy; the Chief, the Super-Chief, the El Capitan go by every day, but these celebrated expresses never pause there. No passenger trains do—only an occasional freight. Up on the highway, there are two filling stations, one of which doubles as a meagerly supplied grocery store, while the other does extra duty as a cafe—Hartman's Cafe, where Mrs. Hartman, the proprietress, dispenses sandwiches, coffee, soft drinks, and 3.2 beer. (Holcomb, like all the rest of Kansas, is "dry.")

And that, really, is all. ...

Until one morning in mid-November of 1959, few Americans—in fact, few Kansans—had ever heard of Holcomb. Like the waters of the river, like the motorists on the highway, and like the yellow trains streaking down the Santa Fe tracks, drama, in the shape of exceptional happenings, had never stopped there. The inhabitants of the village, numbering two hundred and seventy, were satisfied that this should be so, quite content to exist inside ordinary life—to work, to hunt, to watch television, to attend school socials, choir practice, meetings of the 4-H Club. But then, in the earliest hours of that morning in November, a Sunday morning, certain foreign sounds impinged on the normal Holcomb noises—on the keening hysteria of coyotes, the dry scrape of scuttling tumbleweed, the racing, receding wail of locomotive whistles. At the time, not a soul in sleeping Holcomb heard them—four shotgun blasts that, all told, ended six human lives. But afterward the townspeople, theretofore sufficiently unfearful of each other to seldom trouble to lock their doors, found fantasy re-creating them over and again— those sombre explosions that stimulated fires of mistrust, in the glare of which many old neighbors viewed each other strangely, and as strangers.

ACTIVITY

Using your learner portfolio, write a short response to this text.

Remember that, to do well in Paper 1, it is important to focus on the assessment criteria. When writing your analysis of this text, focus on Criterion A (Understanding and interpretation) and Criterion B (Analysis and evaluation). The guiding question can help you focus on key elements of a text, and this can aid your interpretation and evaluation.

Here are some examples of questions you might ask which are linked to Criterion A:

- How well do you understand the text? What conclusions can you make about it?
- How far can you support your ideas with examples from the text?
- Are you able to see the text's purpose, as well as its intended audience?
- To what extent do the words or images used contribute to the meaning of the text?

Here are some questions you might ask for Criterion B:

- How far have you analysed and evaluated features in the text?
- How successful are the author's choices in conveying meaning? How are you measuring this success in relation to the text's intended audience?
- How important is the context to the effectiveness of the text?
- What are the most effective features in the text?

Paper 1: Guided textual analysis (SL/HL)

Community

This passage appears to be a description of a small community in Texas. But although Capote was from the Deep South of the US, he was considered an outsider by those who lived in Holcomb. Do you think his tone is condescending in this passage? Or is it more sympathetic than some of his critics have claimed?

Now read the following facts about the novel from which the extract was taken:

- The extract is the opening of Truman Capote's famous book *In Cold Blood*.
- The book is frequently referred to as a 'non-fiction novel'.
- It was published in the United States in 1966.
- It describes the murders of four members of the Clutter family in Holcomb, Kansas.
- Capote was already a famous journalist and novelist when he decided to travel to the town to report on the killings.
- He researched the book for four years.
- He was accompanied by his childhood friend Harper Lee, whose most famous novel, *To Kill a Mockingbird*, is considered one of the most influential novels of the 20th century.
- *In Cold Blood* was controversial because many people felt Capote was too sympathetic towards the murderers, Dick Hickock and Perry Smith; there were also claims that Capote did not always describe what really happened.
- It is one of the highest-selling true crime books ever written.
- Capote enjoyed considerable fame and fortune after the book was published, but he struggled to cope with this success; his alcoholism and drug addiction became worse, contributing to his death, at the age of 59, in 1984.
- Although there were posthumous publications, *In Cold Blood* was the last full-length book he wrote in his lifetime.
- Capote's celebrity continues, with two movies about him – *Capote* (2005) and *Infamous* (2006) – receiving critical praise.

ACTIVITY

How do these facts change your interpretation of the extract from *In Cold Blood*?

Finding out about a text, and about the issues and events that helped shape a writer's work, can deepen your appreciation of his or her choices. But your initial responses to the text, without this context, are valuable, and should be noted and reflected on in your learner portfolio.

Here is how the murders were reported in the *New York Times* on 16 November 1959:

Wealthy Farmer, 3 Of Family Slain

Holcomb, Kan., Nov. 15 (UPI)—A wealthy wheat farmer, his wife and their two young children were found shot to death today in their home. They had been killed by shotgun blasts at close range after being bound and gagged.

The father, 48-year-old Herbert W. Clutter, was found in the basement with his son, Kenyon, 15. His wife Bonnie, 45, and a daughter, Nancy, 16, were in their beds.

There were no signs of a struggle, and nothing had been stolen. The telephone lines had been cut.

"This is apparently the case of a psychopathic killer," Sheriff Earl Robinson said.

Mr. Clutter was founder of the Kansas Wheat Growers Association. In 1954, President Eisenhower appointed him to the Federal Farm Credit Board, but he never lived in Washington.

The board represents the twelve farm credit districts in the country. Mr. Clutter served from December, 1953, until April, 1957. He declined a reappointment.

He was also a local member of the Agriculture Department's Price Stabilization Board and was active with the Great Plains Wheat Growers Association.

The Clutter farm and ranch cover almost 1,000 acres in one of the richest wheat areas.

Mr. Clutter, his wife and daughter were clad in pajamas. The boy was wearing blue jeans and a T-shirt.

The bodies were discovered by two of Nancy's classmates, Susan Kidwell and Nancy Ewalt.

Sheriff Robinson said the last reported communication with Mr. Clutter took place last night about 9:30 P.M., when the victim called Gerald Van Vleet, his business partner, who lives near by. Mr. Van Vleet said the conversation had concerned the farm and ranch.

Two daughters were away. They are Beverly, a student at Kansas University, and Mrs. Donald G. Jarchow of Mount Carroll, Ill.

New York Times

KEY CONCEPT

Community

Notice how two very different interpretations of the same event can both be 'true'. It can be a constructive process to look at stories currently in the news, and reflect on how they are represented from different perspectives, depending on who is reporting them.

ACTIVITY

1 To what extent do you believe that Capote's text is representative of what happened in Holcomb?

2 Which words and phrases used by Capote do you think are clearly interpretative or subjective?

3 Which words and phrases used by Capote do you think are objective and non-interpretative?

4 Which description of the crime is the most trustworthy? Why?

5 Which text is the most enjoyable to read? Why? Does this matter?

The representation of reality is, to some extent, subjective. But the value of that representation can be judged by how far texts withstand the tests of space and time. Evaluating the resilience of the texts you study is an essential part in developing as a student of language and literature. It is a key skill for Paper 1, and also for other areas of your IB course.

REFLECT

Context can be a very useful way of bringing greater depth to your textual analysis. But another view is that knowing a lot about the author may obscure the text's meaning. After completing this activity, which view do you agree with, and why?

1

Analysing visual non-fiction texts

Look at the following four images and record your first thoughts in your learner portfolio.

- What words and phrases resonate with you? Why?
- Are these advertisements offensive or provocative?
- What do you think the British Army hoped to achieve with this campaign?

Advertisements come in many different forms, but those in print tend to follow established conventions, with the following common features.

Visual narrative: Because we respond strongly to stories, advertisements will try to include a photograph or an image that creates a narrative in the reader's mind. How have these advertisements tried to do this?

Copy: The copy is the words used in the advertisement. What impact do you think the words in these adverts were intended to have? Does this differ from the impact they had on you? Explain your response.

Tagline: This is the catchphrase, or memorable saying, that the advertisers want you to remember after the advertisement is no longer visible.

Signature: This can include the product's name, and also its logo. What are the signatures in these advertisements?

Slogan: This is the phrase used by a product to promote brand awareness. What does the slogan for this 'product' convey to you?

KEY CONCEPT

Identity

To what extent do you think these advertisements are criticising the young? Are they stereotyping young adults – often referred to as 'millennials' – with negative associations? Or are they subverting them? To what extent do you think the gender and ethnic balance in the advertisements is another deliberate recruitment strategy?

ACTIVITY

Look at the British Army campaign advertisements again. Here are three guiding questions that you could use with these images. Put these questions in order of preference, and then explain your choices. Using your learner portfolio to record your thoughts.

1 In what ways do the images used create a narrative in the reader's mind?

2 Discuss the different features used in these texts to persuade the reader to join the armed forces.

3 How do these text types challenge preconceptions of what the armed services are looking for in recruits?

Now write three paragraphs answering each question. In each of these paragraphs, try to focus on:

- how to organise your answer, ensuring that balance is given to each image (Criterion C)

- the language, including tone, and appropriate terminology you should use (Criterion D).

The following aspects of your answer could address Criterion C:

- How much time have you spent planning your answer?

- Have you got a clear understanding of what your 'argument', or angle, will be in analysing the text?

- Is your analysis coherent, and does it address the major themes and the key features?

- How much has the guiding question helped you bring into focus what you are going to write about – and what you are *not* going to write about?

- Do you know what your opening and concluding paragraphs are going to be?

ACTIVITY (CONTINUED)

Here are some aspects of your answer which could address Criterion D:

- What key features can you refer to in your analysis?
- Is the language in the text specific to a particular semantic field (clusters of words that relate to a specific topic)?
- What terminology are you going to apply in your analysis?
- If the language in the text is complex and nuanced, how will you ensure that your vocabulary matches it?

ACTIVITY

There are four images in the British Army's recruitment campaign. Try to improve your understanding of the four key criteria for Paper 1 by focusing on just *one* of the images, and writing four short responses which focus on *each* of the criteria. You might want to use the following table to help you.

Advert	Criterion	Example questions to ask of the text
Binge gamers: Your army needs you and your drive	Criterion A: Understanding and interpretation	What is the literal meaning of the text? What subtleties are there in the text? How do the design features affect your understanding and interpretation of the text?
Phone zombies: Your army needs you and your focus	Criterion B: Analysis and evaluation	Does the image of the soldier conflict with the words used? What is the effect? Why does the advertisement contrast 'zombie' with 'focus', and what is the effect?
Snowflakes: Your army needs you and your compassion	Criterion C: Focus and organisation	What is more important: the image or the words? Do they deliberately conflict? Which points are you going to prioritise and why?
Me Me Me millennials: Your army needs you and your self-belief	Criterion D: Language	How would you describe the use of emotive language in this advertisement? Are there any nuances to the use of language in this text? How will you draw those out in your analysis?

Working on one criterion at a time can help you to develop a disciplined and balanced understanding of them. But remember that your essay should cover each criterion equally, even though it can be tempting to focus on those you are more comfortable exploring.

Animated advertisements

Businesses promote themselves and their products in newspapers and magazines, in brochures, on billboards, on the radio, television and in the cinema. Printed options – such as leaflets, inserts and flyers – continue to be popular. In most developed societies, wherever people gather there will be advertisements–in shop windows, on walls, anywhere that is visible–but advertisers have to work hard to attract attention.

The internet has allowed companies to innovate and evolve their advertising, and to engage people in different ways. Becoming a critical reader of the context you work, walk and talk in is an essential part of living in a modern, interactive environment. Working out what is true, and what isn't, is a vital life skill.

You have already considered the advertisements for the British Army. You will now explore a very different advertising campaign, for Dutch company WeTransfer, made by WeAreCognitive.

Here is some contextual information abut the campaign:

WeAreCognitive are 'whiteboard animators' who provide visual narratives – usually with animated explainer videos and infographics – to tell stories, explain ideas and promote brands. They teamed up with WeTransfer to articulate that company's story to current and potential clients. Their video builds on each part of WeTransfer's development, culminating in one final image at the end. They write this about themselves:

> 'WeTransfer makes tools to move ideas. Founded in 2009 in Amsterdam as a simple, well-designed file sharing service for the creative community, WeTransfer has grown to include tools that scale across the creative spectrum … with 50 million monthly users and over a billion files sent each month.'

WeTransfer invest heavily in the arts and creative industries.

On the next page you can see the final image from the WeTransfer video, created by WeAreCognitive.

You may be given a choice of two visual texts in Paper 1, and these may have multiple elements, like this WeTransfer image.

Analysing texts like this requires different strategies from those you might use for single image advertisements, but there are some things that are the same.

Remember, all texts are trying to construct – and convey – meaning. Businesses want you to engage with their product and, if their advertising works well, to purchase it. Some will go further and encourage you to buy into their values – you will then be more likely to remain loyal to the brand beyond a single transaction.

If you find that the text is difficult to read and interpret, that could be the fault of the author or designer, and you would be able to explore this in your analysis. However, it could be that you have not spent enough time analysing the text, or that it is deliberately complex or ambiguous. For Paper 1, you should allow yourself enough time to work out what the narrative is.

The following notes were written by Max, a student in the second year of studying the IB Diploma. He took 30 minutes to write them, which might seem like a lot of time, but for a complex text like this it is time well spent: writing the essay afterwards was then much quicker and more straightforward.

Max's notes on the image from the WeTransfer video

The bird with WE on it: We/WeTransfer - inclusive, and it is a story.

The main frame of the graphic is a non-descript street: America?

Read from left to right, from top to bottom: so … so the anchor text is 'Beautifully Obvious' and then going down, and to the right: what do the images convey?

They are keen to promote inclusivity: there is a racial and gender balance here which will have been consciously thought through, but so too will the messages: People first, Creativity second, Technology third … is that believable for a tech company? Where is profit?

The four heads below the transmitter signals seem like a folk band, but beneath them = images of a movie clapperboard, a camera, and a musical note, all symbols of creativity: what does that convey? What facial expressions do they have? Happy, content, together.

The symbols below them are universal semiotics for cancelled or prohibited actions, but here they are floating between a young woman with laptop and an older, male laptop user, and they have 'banner ads', 'pop ups' and 'nonsense' barred. Why?

Two women in the groundfloor flat appear to painting - this is a motif across this image: symbols of creativity, and wending its way between them is a banner, circuitous but unthreatening as its message: 'get in and stay in your flow 1/3 to creatives & causes' … what does this mean? Again, the crowd sitting on the steps in the bottom right are ethnically and religiously diverse, displaying obvious symbols of creativity ('Hamlet', a man playing a guitar), and also 'progressive' politics: the 'peace' sign, the man with an exclamation mark on his jersey being filmed. Funded activism?

There seems to be an advertising space with ⅓ at the middle: it isn't clear what this signifies, but it seems that, again, through the use of iconic images, such as a ballerina, a camera, an artist with an easel, the company donates signficant $$$$$ of what it makes to creative industry.

To the left of the image there is another ethnically diverse crowd apparently watching some full screen advertising on a rooftop area, presumably to indicate that WeTransfer are involved in this side of the creative industries. Sense of community.

Here is a more focused description of their finance: to reassure investors, customers? Reliable. Broke even in 2014; 2015 raised $25m. Not immediately clear what 'zag' means, but the figures are similar to the artist Keith Haring (?): non-conformity? street? 1 figure - in a more creative 'bubble' (?) is running, not walking, as the other figure appears to be doing (and against a rigid, metalic panel). Not clear about this: develop?

Ad revenues heading in the same direction, and the dollar bill at the arrow's head indicates that money is playing a starring role, especially as it is lit up by the lights around it.

The $25m figure appears on top of a building which is suggestive of a funfair 'high striker'/test of strength game. Lots of images affirm this: roller coaster on the right hand side, hot air balloon with 'We Present' written on its side, and the big wheel with 'Free MA experience design' written on it to poss. promote another aspect of the company's selflessness. All these funfair images - fun. Community. Spirit of adventure.

Unclear who Nelly Ben Hayoun or Gilles Peterson are, or what the Uni of the Underground and Worldwide FM, and the images at the high centre - which appear to be various (differently able, and ethnically diverse) people in front of tablets and cell phones, which could suggest that this is a company which has fully embraced mobile tech?

Rising sun at the centre of the image is a strong symbol of hope, and emblazoned with the number of users they now have (43m).

End where we started: 'beautifully obvious'. Although not all of the images are clear, it has to be remembered that this is a screenshot, and that with narration the 'story' being told will be obvious. Is it beautiful? Obvious? Conclude with 'eye of beholder'?

TIP
We remember things in different ways. Mnemonics – a system which uses the first letters of key words to create an easily memorised word – can be useful. If you have difficulty remembering the assessment criteria then perhaps the first letters of the key words might help:

UI (Understanding and interpretation)
AE (Analysis and evaluation)
FO (Focus and organisation)
L (Language).

Taken together UI–AE–FO–L has a sing-song quality and can be recalled easily. If other mnemonics work for you – then use them!

How well has Max written these notes, to give a good basis for an analytical essay on the WeTransfer text? How would you organise these notes to form a coherent and sustained argument? Does Max focus on some assessment criteria more than others?

ACTIVITY

Before you read Max's essay, look at the guiding question: what key words would you highlight? Discuss your choices, and decide how you would focus on these words in relation to the image.

Peer-assessment

Max took 90 minutes to write the following analysis of the WeAreCognitive advertisement. As you read it, annotate his essay to find out how often he has addressed each of the four assessment criteria.

Guiding question:

In what ways do the elements in the image convey the narrative the creators intended?

Max's analysis of the image from the WeTransfer video

WeAreCognitive are an advertising company; WeTransfer are a tech company that transports large electronic files between servers. The image they have created is a complex narrative (the 'strapline' has 'A WeTransfer Story' if we were in any doubt about this) that not only seeks to explain WeTransfer's services, but also their values. It is perhaps not a coincidence that both companies share one thing in common: they both include the inclusive pronoun 'we' in their names. As we will see from analysing the image, this emphasis on collaboration - as well as inclusivity and diversity - are at the heart of the messages they are both trying to sell.

The image is almost completely made up of symbols, and perhaps because of that the narrative WeAreCognitive is trying to write can appear too contrived and complex. It is not, despite the banner advertising at the top of the image, 'beautifully obvious'. The setting appears to be a mid-West American town from its cartoon architecture, but it could just as easily be seen as a film set in Hollywood, with Ferris Wheels, big dippers, hot air balloons, fairgrounds, and even outsized figures overseeing everything like modern, techie gods, each holding a different mobile device.

The various symbols foregrounded have a number of qualities in common with each other: the pigeon, the balloon, the transmitter, the train track and the big wheel all have connotations of movement and agency, which of course ties in with WeTransfer's business model. As we read the image from left to right we begin to make sense of what is attempting to be conveyed by the two companies, and also what is being relegated to something less important.

It is clear that what WeTransfer is trying to emphasise is community, creativity and inclusivity. In an age of identity politics this is clearly appealing to a younger and politically engaged client base. What they are making more modest claims for is the less cool subject of money, and we have to look quite hard to find out information in this graphic about how they operate, and whether they are commercially successful. In fact, WeTransfer seem to suggest that an operating profit is not very important to them at all: 'People first, creativity second, technology third' are their stated priorities. But the reader may be entitled to ask if this is really true.

The image is extremely busy: it is filled with people, with all ages, ethnicities and body types represented. And every one of these figures seems to be involved in either something creative, or enjoyable, or both. The irony is that for a company to quickly convey what being creative is they have to often revert to non-creative, or clichéd, symbols. So, for example, dance is symbolised by a ballerina; photography is symbolised by a camera; acting is reduced to someone apparently performing 'Hamlet', painting is personified as someone with a brush holding a palette. Diversity and inclusivity are similarly predictable with as wide a range of demographic as is possible to fit into one image. It is understandable - and admirable - why a company wants to promote such values, but it is difficult not to conclude that this rather lacks the originality that they place so much importance on.

The various texts that are included to articulate messages that cannot be conveyed by images alone, are also equally lacking in creativity: 'get in and stay in your flow' is something from a 1960s hippy songbook, and it is no coincidence that this idealistic message also flows into something more materialistic: $\frac{1}{3}$ to creatives & causes'. Those causes are vague, and if they were made clear might put off some investors: is the peace sign indicating that they give to the campaign for nuclear disarmament? Other words such as 'zag', or 'Free MA Experience Design' are almost meaningless without greater context.

As we continue to read around the frame we end at the bottom line: money. Here WePresent are rather reticent about details: WeTransfer broke even in 2014 and raised $25m in 2015, but you would have to look elsewhere for information about pricing and profits. It is as if such prosaic issues should not stain the utopian message the image is trying to convey. Finally, we reach the beginning of the story, and it ends with a rising (or setting) sun, indicating hope, presumably, as well as something which is driven home by the blunt statement of '43 million users'. Here, in that final image of sunshine on the horizon you also have the marriage of the inescapable fact that a company can dedicate as much time and energy to investing in good causes, and putting people first, but unless it delivers with customers none of that will make much difference to whether it succeeds or fails. It seems that, commercially, WeTransfer works. Artistically, WeAreCognitive could do better.

Peer-assessment

After reading Max's analysis, talk to a partner about how you would grade it using the assessment criteria.

Once you have graded Max's analysis of the WeTransfer video image and agreed on a mark for each criterion, write some comments justifying why you awarded those marks and why any marks were lost.

Criterion	Your comments to support your mark
Criterion A: Understanding and interpretation	
Criterion B: Analysis and evaluation	
Criterion C: Focus and organisation	
Criterion D: Language	
Total mark out of 20	
What were the strengths of the essay?	
Which areas needed further improvement?	
What overall comments would you make?	

Photographs

As ownership of smartphones increases, we are taking – and sharing – more photographs than ever before. We look at more images every day than in the past, and in many ways we are becoming more visually literate. Most of the images we take ourselves, or view on social media, are taken to capture a moment or an experience. How skilled are you in analysing a carefully composed image and creating a coherent argument? Which entry points do you use? What is the focus for your analysis?

Gregory Crewdson is an American photographer whose work is highly structured. Each of his images deliberately tries to convey a narrative.

ACTIVITY

Look at this image by Gregory Crewdson and write a ten-point plan on the accompanying guiding question.

KEY CONCEPT

Creativity

Reading is a creative act: we bring our own interpretations, associations and preconceptions to every image and paragraph we read. This image is very carefully constructed and, although it was created by the photographer, it could be argued that it is the reader who completes the narrative.

Guiding question:

In what ways does the imagery used in this photograph create a narrative in the reader's mind?

Asking the right questions

When analysing a text, you should start by making an initial plan, and by asking yourself a number of questions. Interrogate the image in the hope that most – if not all – of the questions you have asked can be answered before you start writing.

Crewdson's image is outwardly naturalistic: it seems to be an innocent winter scene of an ordinary suburb in the United States. But look closer and questions begin to be raised:

- Is it significant that it is winter, and that snow has fallen?
- Why has the car stopped in the middle of the road? Is it because of the traffic lights? Or is it because of the woman in the far right: is there a connection between her and the driver?
- The car at the centre of the image seems to be the only vehicle that has moved recently. Even the bus has 'Not in Service' lit up. Why?
- This image suggests coldness; why then is the window above the restaurant open?
- Is it significant that the lights are on amber? Why?
- Is this early morning or early evening? Does it matter what time it is?
- Apart from the woman and the driver, there appears to be only one other person in the scene: what role is he playing?
- How significant is it that the movie playing in the cinema is *Brief Encounter*? How could this title be applied to the whole image?
- The scene is set on 'Melville Street': is this an allusion to Herman Melville, author of *Moby Dick*?
- There are very few words visible in this image: 'brief encounter', 'restaurant', 'tattoo': what do these convey to you? Transience? Permanence?

- How would you describe the mood of this image? Support your ideas with evidence from the image.

- Think about the context: the film *Brief Encounter* was made in 1945, but the cars, and the clothes of the two people in the image suggest that this scene takes place much later in the 20th century. But when? There appear to be no advertisements that could locate it in a specific period, and no obviously modern references. Can you put a rough date to it? If not, is this deliberate?

Asking such questions makes you engage with the text in a number of different ways. Remember, though, that there may not be any definite answers: the ambiguity and mystery of Crewdson's images are partly what makes them so appealing and popular.

It can also be helpful to think about analysing a text using a series of different aspects. These could include:

- purpose
- style and structure
- audience
- meaning.

If you consider these aspects of a text, then your analysis is more likely to be well balanced and detailed.

Sample student response

Let's look at how one student, Tung-Yat, attempted to answer the guiding question for the Crewdson image. Read his essay, and the teacher's comments.

Good, clear start	**Purpose**
	This image seems designed to unsettle us. Although it evokes what appears to be
Establishes 'surface' meaning quickly, before going on to state that there are deeper interpretations possible	an innocent winter scene in suburban America, it is only when we start looking closer that something different – and darker – begins to emerge. It is a mysterious scene, but we can't help thinking that it was the photographer's intention to create that mystery, to not provide us with answers to the questions we have. If this was his
Concise and direct way of concluding first paragraph	purpose then he has succeeded.
	Style and structure
Good topic sentence: links with the point before and then goes on to make important claims about the image	The overall tone of the image builds on this sense of mystery, but adds sadness and regret, and one of the key themes that promotes this atmosphere is the representation of time. Snow has fallen, but apart from the car – which we see from its tyre tracks has recently travelled – nothing seems to have moved. We are caught between states: even the traffic lights are stuck between green for 'go' and red for 'stop'. Time is
Again: good, concise final sentence to this paragraph	suspended here.
	It is interesting that the movie being shown in the cinema is 'Brief Encounter': this
Shows good general knowledge of context: deepens analysis	film was first released in the 1940s, so why is it playing now? Is it to highlight the brief encounter between the driver in the car and the woman dressed in red sitting in the restaurant? Who is the third man, standing outside the cinema? Her husband? Her lover waiting for her to meet him? We will never know. In what is
Perhaps too many rhetorical questions: the point has been made	clearly ambiguous and intentional, it is not made clear by the photographer if this is early morning or early evening.

There is, though, a clear narrative created here. The lighting is suggestive of twilight, of fading day, and perhaps fading hope. Each of the people in this frozen scene are alone, waiting, perhaps for change, or for each other. There is the irony that although it is a scene about transience – the snow will melt, the lights will change, the car will move – it remains a still, a moment frozen in time. Each image contributes to the overall impression that this is one metaphor for the passing of time. But this is a narrative with no beginning, middle or end, and no chance of a plot developing either, unless the viewer does it themselves.

> Important to state at the start of this paragraph

> Good use of appropriate technical vocabulary

Apart from the restaurant it seems the only shop open is selling tattoos, which are so often the symbols of permanent love, at odds with the other side of the street. But they are also suggestive of sailors and the sea, of escape. It is perhaps not a coincidence that the scene takes place on Melville Street, evoking Herman Melville, author of 'Moby Dick', which itself is a story of fading dreams, of people escaping their pasts. There are also clear comparisons to the work of Edward Hopper, both in terms of subject matter and tone: the woman in the restaurant could have been lifted directly from one of Hopper's canvases. Nothing, it seems, is a coincidence in this image.

> Sophisticated analysis

Audience

Given that it is carefully structured, and has clear cultural references, this image is aimed at a visually sophisticated and literary audience. It makes demands of us, both in terms of what it is referencing, but also which themes it is exploring. The passing of time, the loss of love, isolation, despair: these are themes which are difficult to think about, and when we see them brought to life with the clarity of a movie, as in this image, they become even more challenging. The photographer wants us to spend a lot of time reading this image, which is very different from how we experience most photographs. In fact, photographs, more than any other art form, are characterised by transience: they catch a moment in time in a way that a poem, a novel or a painting do not even try to do. This image subverts that convention and, in this respect, it is closer to a movie or a painting. It looks like a stage set, and the characters involved are actors being directed by the artist.

> Good awareness of purpose and audience

> Again, good use of vocabulary

Meaning

There is no clear meaning in this image, and that, perhaps, is its point. It is ambiguous and mysterious, much like life itself. We will never know if the woman is waiting for the man in the car, or the man outside the cinema: did she have a date to see 'Brief Encounter' but has decided not to go? Is it her husband in the car, brake lights on, wondering why she is there? The image asks us to think about such matters, but also to contemplate the mood of the piece, which is melancholic, and filled with the regret of the passing day, rather than the new morning. Snow has fallen, and will soon melt away, and with it, perhaps, the dreams of the characters we catch sight of for a moment.

> Needs rather more clarity here

> Again, rather vague in this final paragraph, and this is not the place to start making wide, philosophical points

> Not a strong final sentence; it is too ambiguous and not evaluative. Reads more like literary text than analytical.

Peer-assessment

Assess this essay by Tung-Yat. Use the assessment criteria for Paper 1 to help you decide where he picks up marks, and where he loses them.

Teacher's overall comment

This shows a good understanding of the text's meaning; in places this is highly sophisticated writing, but it can also be unfocused, and it concludes in a rather vague manner by making very general points about life, rather than the image under analysis.

What feedback would you give him to suggest how he could improve this essay?

Criterion A	Understanding and interpretation	How well has the student understood the main ideas behind the text? Is the interpretation valid?	5 marks
Criterion B	Analysis and evaluation	How perceptive and sustained is the analysis? Is the evaluation balanced?	5 marks
Criterion C	Focus and organisation	Is there a clear and sustained focus to the analysis? Is the essay well organised throughout?	5 marks
Criterion D	Language	Is the language sophisticated, and is the technical vocabulary used appropriately?	5 marks
Total		**What final mark would you give to this essay?**	**20 marks**

ACTIVITY

Here is a possible guiding question for the Crewdson photograph:

In what ways does the use of symbolism in this photograph help the reader to create a coherent narrative?

Now write *two* more guiding questions for this image, focusing on different entry points.

REFLECT

Read Tung-Yat's essay, and the teacher's comments, again. How would you analyse this image differently? Where could you improve on this analysis?

Webpages

Look at the following webpage fromWikipedia.

WIKIPEDIA
The Free Encyclopedia

Project page   Talk

Read   Edit   View history   Search Wikipedia   🔍

Wikipedia:Why Wikipedia is so great

From Wikipedia, the free encyclopedia

This page is an essay.
It contains the advice or opinions of one or more Wikipedia contributors. This page is not one of Wikipedia's policies or guidelines, as it has not been thoroughly vetted by the community. Some essays represent widespread norms; others only represent minority viewpoints.

As you read and edit Wikipedia, at some point you may ask yourself: "Just **why is Wikipedia so awesome**? What accounts for its enormous growth and success?" In order to answer this question, some great people have written some explanations and arguments on this page. For comparison, see also why Wikipedia is not so great, and Wikipedia:Replies to common objections. You can then arrive at a well-informed conclusion thereafter.

Shortcuts
WP:WWISG
WP:WSG

Contents [hide]
1 Editing
2 Organisation
3 Comprehensiveness and depth
4 Vandalism
5 Success factors
6 Additional comments
7 See also
8 References and notes

The English edition of Wikipedia has grown to 5,908,317 articles, equivalent to over 2,500 print volumes of the *Encyclopædia Britannica*. Including all language editions, Wikipedia has over 50 million articles,[1] equivalent to over 19,000 print volumes.

Main page
Contents
Featured content
Current events
Random article
Donate to Wikipedia
Wikipedia store

Interaction
Help
About Wikipedia
Community portal
Recent changes
Contact page

Tools
What links here
Related changes
Upload file
Special pages
Permanent link
Page information
Wikidata item

Print/export
Create a book
Download as PDF
Printable version

Languages   ⚙
Español
Français
Bahasa Melayu
日本語
ภาษาไทย
Português
Русский
文A 5 more
🖉 Edit links

Editing   [edit]

- Wikipedia articles are very easy to edit. Anyone can click the "edit" link and edit an article. Obtaining formal peer review for edits is not necessary since the review is a communal function here and everyone who reads an article and corrects it is a reviewer. Essentially, Wikipedia is *self-correcting* – over time, articles improve from a multitude of contributions. There is an entire infrastructure for people seeking comments, or other opinions on editorial matters, and as a result, Wikipedia has got "consensus-seeking" down to a fine art. We prefer (in most cases) that people just go in and make changes they deem necessary; the community is by and large quick to respond to dubious edits (if any) and either revert or question them. This is very efficient; our efforts seem more *constructive* than those on similar projects (not to mention any names).
- Tim Berners-Lee, the inventor of the World Wide Web, repeatedly mentions in his book *Weaving the Web* that the web has grown into a medium that is much easier to read than to edit. He envisaged the web as a much more collaborative medium than it currently is, and thought that the browser should also function as an editor. Wiki-based sites are closer to his vision. In fact, the first web browser was also a web editor.
- While traditional encyclopaedias might be revised annually, Wikipedia's current affairs articles, as well as their older articles being edited, are updated thousands of times an hour. That's a big deal if your interest is in current affairs, recent science, pop culture, or any other field that changes rapidly.
- Errors to Wikipedia can be corrected within seconds, rather than within months as with a paper encyclopaedia. When someone sees something wrong in an article, they can simply fix it themselves. If they cannot correct it, they can "tag" the problem to attract the attention of other editors. Compare that to the slow, tedious process required to report and fix a problem in a paper encyclopaedia.
- On Wikipedia, there are no required topics and no one is setting assignments. That means that anyone can find part of the encyclopaedia they're interested in and add to it immediately (if they can do better than what's already there). This increases motivation and keeps things fun.
- Wikipedia is open content, released under the GNU Free Documentation License. Knowing this encourages people to contribute; they know it's a public project that everyone can use.
- Where else can you get lovely articles on a such-and-such town or so-and-so bizarre hobby written by actual residents/practitioners? (Of course, some view this as a curse.) Many articles on Wikipedia will likely never have an entry in a paper encyclopaedia.
- The use of talk pages. If an article doesn't cover something, you can ask about it.
- Requesting articles. If any article you try to find isn't here, you can request it.
- Most editors on Wikipedia are amateurs. However, many contributors on specific matters are professionals or have firsthand knowledge on the subjects they write about. These contributions allow many scholars to gather information to aid them in research matters, and even just for everyday general knowledge.

Organisation [edit]

- Wikipedia has almost no bureaucracy; one might say it has none at all. But it isn't total anarchy. There are social pressures and community norms, but perhaps that by itself doesn't constitute bureaucracy, because anybody *can* go in and make any changes they feel like making. And other people generally like it when they do. So there aren't any bottlenecks; anyone can come in and make progress on the project at any time. The project is self-policing. Editorial oversight is more or less continuous with writing, which seems, again, very efficient. But in some cases, there will be "locked" articles, to prevent vandalism, on subjects like the President of the United States.
- Life isn't fair, and internet communities usually aren't fair either. If some random administrator doesn't like you on an internet forum, you'll be gone from there fairly quickly, because they run the place so they make the rules. But on Wikipedia, everyone can edit by default. Even if you're a bad speller, or even if you're too young to legally tell us your name, or even if you have a controversial point of view, or even if you hate Wikipedia, as long as you can improve our articles you are welcome to contribute. Of course, we ban people who are impossibly destructive, but even then we will sometimes give them a second chance. We have over 1,100 administrators who check each other's decisions.

Comprehensiveness and depth [edit]

- Wikipedia is by far the world's largest encyclopedia; it is the largest, most comprehensive, and most accessible compilation of knowledge to exist in the history of the human race. With the English Wikipedia now having more than five million articles, it is already well over twenty times the size of what was previously the world's largest encyclopedia (the largest edition of the *Encyclopedia Britannica*, which contains 65,000 articles). With each new article, information is becoming more accessible than it ever has before.
- Wikipedia's neutral point of view policy makes it an excellent place to gain a quick understanding of controversial topics. Want a good overview of the Arab–Israeli conflict but only have ten minutes to spare? Wondering what all the fuss is about in Kashmir or what the pro/con arguments are about stem cell research? Wikipedia is a great place to start.
- Wikipedia is not paper, and that is a good thing because articles are not strictly limited in size as they are with paper encyclopedias.
- Articles steadily become more polished as they develop, particularly if there is one person working on an article with reasonable regularity (inclining others to help the original author). There are some articles we can all point to that started out life mediocre at best and are now at least somewhat better than mediocre. If the project lasts many years, thus attracting many more people (as is reasonable to assume), these very articles have the ability to improve greatly over the time span that they exist.
- Wikipedia attracts highly intelligent, articulate people (with the exception of repeat vandals) with some time on their hands. Moreover, there are some experts who contribute to the articles. Over time, the huge amount of solid work done by hobbyists and experts alike will inevitably build upon itself, therefore greatly improving Wikipedia's body of information. As a result, Wikipedia is an intellectual community, confident that the quality of Wikipedia articles will, if not yet, become high.
- Wikipedia, having contributors from many areas of the world, provides its readers with a "world view" that could not be provided simply by few contributors from a limited region. This also serves to eliminate cultural bias in articles.
- To use an extended metaphor, Wikipedia is very fertile soil for knowledge. As encyclopedia articles grow, they can attract gardeners who will weed and edit them, while the discussion between community members provides light to help their growth. By consistent effort and nourishment, Wikipedia articles can become beautiful and informative.
- The sheer amount of information in one search on Wikipedia compared to other search engines, which often provide little useful knowledge on each of hundreds, if not thousands, of results, can be found more concisely (and perhaps safely) than through traditional means.

Vandalism [edit]

- Wikipedia, *by its very nature*, resists destructive edits (known as Vandalism). **All previous revisions of an article are saved and stored**. Once vandalism is committed, in three or four clicks we can have it reverted. Think about it: in order to vandalize a page extensively, you would probably need around thirty seconds (unless it involved simply blanking the page). Compare that to the five to ten seconds it takes to revert an article. Couple that with IP blocking, dedicated souls, and an intelligent robot that monitors edits to the encyclopedia, and you have a solid resistance against destructive edits.
- Most vandalism involves replacing parts of a passage or deleting a passage and replacing it with something else – very few cases involve introducing misinformation, and even fewer misinformation and hoax edits go through. Wikipedia has a feature that allows an editor to remove an edit with just a few clicks.

Success factors [edit]

- Wikipedia's success mainly depends on its users, the **Wikipedians**.
- In theory, everybody can be a **Wikipedian**, but does the theory hold true in practice?
- The idea is that the Wiki-community of **Wikipedians** is a special group of people who have special characteristics. To account for these special characteristics, we have provided the following factor model:
  - **User factors**
    - Openness
    - Computer skills
    - Motivation
    - Neutrality
    - Flat hierarchy
  - **Knowledge factors**
    - Type of knowledge
    - Fast changing rate
    - Peer review
  - **Technology factors**
    - Easy usability
    - Fast access
    - Infinite reach, multilingual
    - Flexible structure
    - Safe
- All of these factors play together to accomplish the goal of successful knowledge creation and knowledge sharing.
- A study done by the University of Washington found that 8 in 10 college students use Wikipedia as an introduction to finding information for their research.[2]

Additional comments [edit]

- We have a slowly growing source of traffic—and therefore more contributors, and therefore (very possibly, anyway) an increasing rate of article-writing—from Google and Google-using search engines like AOL, Netscape, and a9. The greater the number and quality of Wikipedia articles, the greater the number of people will link to us, and therefore the higher the rankings (and numbers of listings) we'll have on Google. Hence, on Wikipedia "the rich (will) get richer"; or "if we build it, they will come" and in greater and greater numbers.
- Our likelihood of success seems encouragingly high. On January 23, 2003 we reached 100,000 articles, and we have since passed 10,000,000 articles, with over 5,000,000 English articles alone. If Wikipedia hits it big, or even simply continues as it has been, which seems plausible, then all potential articles might be covered... eventually.
- Wikipedia is free. Many online encyclopedias are not.
- It's a good feeling seeing that one's contribution is potentially read by thousands of surfers.
- Wikipedia takes information from other reliable websites and puts it onto one portal. Each piece of information added to a page can be individually cited so readers can find the source and get more information.
- Wikipedia has no set in stone rules, rather, it has the "Five Pillars" which highlight the main principles and guidelines of Wikipedia.

See also [edit]

- Wikipedia:Testimonials
- Wikipedia:Why Wikipedia is not so great
- Wikipedia:Wikipedia is failing
- Wikipedia:Wikipedia is succeeding

References and notes [edit]

1. ^ "Wikistats 2 - Statistics For Wikimedia Projects" . *stats.wikimedia.org*.
2. ^ Nagel, David. "8 in 10 Students Turn to Wikipedia for Research" . *Campus Technology*. Retrieved 15 December 2014.

Paper 1: Guided textual analysis (SL/HL)

Guiding question:

How successfully does the structure of this webpage convey information about Wikipedia?

Now read the following example of an introductory paragraph to an analysis of this webpage, written by a student.

> Wikipedia is a hugely popular online encyclopedia.[1] This webpage, from Wikipedia itself, attempts not only to introduce a general reader to its main features but also to explain why it is so popular. The body text[2] includes a lot of information, but makes use of embedded links[3] that allow the reader – if they are interested – to explore these references. The page is clearly organised,[4] and clearly follows the Wikipedia design features[5] that bring coherence to a vast amount of information. The website also makes use of graphs, as well as statistics, and includes references to trusted commentators, such as Tim Berners-Lee, all of which combine to emphasise the point that Wikipedia is a trusted source of information. As an introduction to Wikipedia this is effective, and the page's organisation is an integral part of its success.

How would you evaluate this introductory paragraph? Here are some points, highlighted in the paragraph, that you might have considered as you were reading.

1   Good, clear opening sentence that shows an awareness of the subject matter.

2   Appropriate use of technical terms.

3   Shows a secure understanding of how the page is organised.

4   Again, confident start which responds directly to the guiding question.

5   Shows good general knowledge of the context of the text.

ACTIVITY

Allow yourself 45 minutes to write an analysis of this webpage that addresses the guiding question. You may want to include the following terms in your answer, where appropriate:

anchor text	panel
body text	symbol
illustration	tabs
link	search
logo	subsections

Remember that you won't be able to address every aspect of the webpage. You should instead focus on the guiding question, and extend your analysis to the most – and least – effective aspects of the design. In your planning, you could evaluate how each section of the essay addresses the guiding question.

Asking questions which are informed by technical terms can help clarify your answer:

• What is the **anchor text**? And why has that been selected to fulfil this function?

• How detailed is the **body text**? Does it successfully convey key information?

• Are there any **illustrations** used to extend meaning? Are they successful?

- Which **links** are included? How evenly are they distributed? How visible are they?

- Does the design employ any **logos**? Are they distinctive? What do they seek to convey?

- Explain how **panels** work in the design. Do they make meaning clearer?

- Are there any unusual or eye-catching **symbols** being used? Explain their function.

- How many **tabs** are used? Where are they included? Do you think they are useful or a distraction?

- Is there a **search** function? Why? What does that say about the size or nature of the website?

- Are there any **social media** or **share** buttons? What do these indicate if present, and what does it say about the text if they are absent)?

Technical terms such as these – like literary terms in a literary essay – will not boost your answer if used simply to show the examiner that you know some key terms. But using them appropriately and thinking of questions which allow you to write a strong response can help you to fulfil Criteria A, B and D.

Letters

Jourdon Anderson was a slave on a plantation in Big Spring, Tennessee for 32 years. In 1864 he and his wife, Amanda, escaped from his owner, Colonel Patrick Henry Anderson, and fled to Ohio. Once a free man, Jourdon started working to earn money and to raise his large family. But not long after the end of the Civil War, Jourdon's former owner wrote to him to ask him to return to the plantation to save his business.

This is Jourdon's reply. It was dictated to Valentine Winters, who was Jourdon's employer, and a leading abolitionist of the time. The letter was published in a local newspaper, but soon gained national exposure when other newspapers across the United States published it. Needless to say, he never did return to help out Patrick Anderson, and indeed went on to live a long life, until his death aged 81, in 1907. He and his wife had 11 children.

7 August 1865

Sir,

I got your letter, and was glad to find that you had not forgotten Jourdon, and that you wanted me to come back and live with you again, promising to do better for me than anybody else can. I have often felt uneasy about you. I thought the Yankees would have hung you long before this, for harboring rebs they found at your house. I suppose they never heard about your going to Colonel Martin's to kill the union soldier that was left by his company in their stable. Although you shot at me twice before I left you, I did not want to hear of your being hurt, and am glad you are still living. It would do me good to go back to the dear old home again, and see Miss Mary and Miss Martha and Allen, Esther, Green, and Lee. Give my love to them all, and tell them I hope we will meet in the better world, if not in this. I would have gone back to see you all when I was working in the Nashville hospital, but one of the neighbors told me that Henry intended to shoot me if he ever got a chance.

I want to know particularly what the good chance is you propose to give me. I am doing tolerably well here. I get $25 a month, with victuals and clothing; have a comfortable home for Mandy – the folks call her Mrs Anderson – and the children – Milly, Jane, and Grundy – go to school and are learning well. The teacher says Grundy has for a preacher. They go to Sunday school, and Mandy and me attend church regularly. We are kindly treated. Sometimes we overhear others saying: "Them coloured people were slaves down in Tennessee." The children feel hurt when they hear such remarks; but I tell them it was no disgrace in Tennessee to belong to Colonel Anderson. Many darkeys would have been proud, as I used to be, to call you master. Now if you will write and say what wages you will give me, I will be better able to decide whether it would be to my advantage to move back again.

As to my freedom, which you say I can have, there is nothing to be gained on that score, as I got my free papers in 1864 from the provost-marshal-general of the department of Nashville. Mandy says she would be afraid to go back without some proof that you were disposed to treat us justly and kindly; and we have concluded to test your sincerity by asking you to send us our wages for the time we served you. This will make us forget and forgive old scores, and rely on your justice and friendship in the future. I served you faithfully for 32 years, and Mandy 20 years. At $25 a month for me, and $2 a week for Mandy, our earnings would amount to $11,680. Add to this the interest for the time our wages have been kept back, and deduct what you paid for our clothing, and three doctor's visits to me, and pulling a tooth for Mandy, and the balance will show what we are in justice entitled to. Please send the money by Adams's Express, in care of V Winters, Esq, Dayton, Ohio. If you fail to pay us for faithful labors in the past, we can have little faith in your promises in the future. We trust the good Maker has opened your eyes to the wrongs which you and your fathers have done to me and my fathers, in making us toil for you for generations without recompense. Here I draw my wages every Saturday night; but in Tennessee there was never any pay-day for the negroes any more than for the horses and cows. Surely there will be a day of reckoning for those who defraud the laborer of his hire.

In answering this letter, please state if there would be any safety for my Milly and Jane, who are now grown up, and both good-looking girls. You know how it was with poor Matilda and Catherine. I would rather stay here and starve – and die, if it come to that – than have my girls brought to shame by the violence and wickedness of their young masters. You will also please state if there has been any schools opened for the coloured children in your neighborhood. The great desire of my life now is to give my children an education, and have them form virtuous habits.

Say howdy to George Carter, and thank him for taking the pistol from you when you were shooting at me.

From your old servant,
Jourdon Anderson

Guiding question:

To what extent does the language used in this letter successfully convey the author's intentions?

What are the author's intentions here? Clearly he is determined not to go back to Colonel Anderson, but this could quite easily have been achieved through not returning Anderson's letter. There was no obligation to reply to him, nor any objective need to write at such length. Clearly, then, Jourdon had a clear purpose in writing this letter. What do you think it was?

- To anger Colonel Anderson?

- To humiliate Colonel Anderson?

- To justify to Jourdon himself why he would not go back?

- To outline the crimes that Colonel Anderson had committed?

- To forgive Colonel Anderson?

- To raise awareness and understanding of slavery?

Answering such questions is important if you are to address the guiding question provided. In highly personal texts, such as letters, diary entries or journals, understanding the tone is important. Reading everything very carefully, and annotating your ideas as you go along, will help you.

Once this has been completed, you will have a number of 'entry points' into Jourdon Anderson's letter.

ACTIVITY

Look at the following words and phrases. What do you think Jourdon's intentions were in choosing these? Once you have read the comments in the right-hand column for 1–10, try to write your own for 11–20. Then go through the letter, marking up words and phrases, and writing your comments next to them.

	Word or phrase	Comments
1	I ... was glad you had not forgotten Jourdon	Why was he glad? And why write about himself in the third person?
2	You wanted me to come back and live with you again, promising to do better for me than anybody else can.	Why tell Anderson what he already knows? Did Jourdon plan to have this published from the start? Is he providing context to other readers?
3	I have often felt uneasy about you.	A short, blunt sentence. 'Uneasy' is an unusual word to use: it seems ambiguous, especially when you read the next few sentences.
4	I thought the Yankees would have hung you long before this	A strong admission, and he is clearly stating that Anderson deserved to die.
5	I suppose they never heard about your going ... stable	Again, a very specific accusation which must have been intended to cause serious problems for Jourdon's former owner.
6	Although you shot me twice before I left you, I did not want to hear of your being hurt.	This says as much about Jourdon as about his former slave owner: the latter is described as murderous, but Jourdon seems forgiving and altruistic.
7	'... see Miss Mary and Miss Martha and Allen ...'	Perhaps Jourdon's respectful tone can be explained here: there are still people close to him who are at risk from Anderson and so he has to be diplomatic at times.
8	I would have gone back to see you all ... Henry intended to shoot me	Again, Jourdon shows that he wants to act selflessly and with compassion, but he also shows that he is aware of the danger he faces.

	Word or phrase	Comments
9	I want to know particularly what the good chance is you propose to give me.	This new paragraph gets to the 'business' of the letter: Jourdon wants financial compensation for the unpaid work he and his family have done for Colonel Anderson. It shows he cannot be taken advantage of.
10	The folks call her Mrs Anderson	This shows that, although the money is important, so is gaining respect for him and his wife from the community.
11	The children – Milly, Jane and Grundy – go to school and are learning well.	
12	Mandy and me attend church regularly.	
13	I tell them it was no disgrace in Tennessee to belong to Colonel Anderson	
14	If you fail to pay us for faithful labors in the past, we can have little faith in your promises in the future.	
15	We trust the good Maker has opened your eyes to the wrongs which you and your fathers have done to me and my fathers.	
16	In Tennessee there was never any pay-day for the negroes any more than for the horses and cows.	
17	Surely there will be a day of reckoning	
18	You know how it was with poor Matilda and Catherine ... girls brought to shame by the violence and wickedness of their young masters.	
19	The great desire of my life is now to give my children an education, and have them form virtuous habits.	
20	Say howdy to George Carter, and thank him for taking the pistol from you when you were shooting at me.	

Sample response

The following paragraph was written by a student in his first year of the English A: Language and Literature course. As you read it, think about:

- how well he has created the appropriate *tone* of a formal essay
- how far he has succeeded in achieving a good balance between establishing the context of the letter and evaluating its impact.

Jourdon's letter to his former slave owner is not only a powerful piece of writing, but it is also highly skilled in its use of language. The former slave had to be diplomatic with Colonel Anderson, because although he clearly had no real intention of returning to work on the plantation, he also had to be aware that those he had to leave behind were still at risk from Anderson and the 'young masters'. He also had to show anyone who read his letter that he was not only free, but was an astute businessman who could no longer be taken advantage of. Finally, he also had to show others, including perhaps himself, that matters such as respect and education mattered as much to him as the money he was asking for before he would consider returning.

The letter is carefully structured, and each part contributes equally to its effectiveness.

ACTIVITY

Think back to your analysis of the Wikipedia webpages earlier in this section. Make some notes on Jourdon Anderson's letter, thinking about questions you could ask that would involve the following terms:

- contrasts
- humour (including irony)
- imagery
- personal
- political
- structure (including paragraphing, sentence length and sentence types)
- tone
- word choice.

Consider carefully how you can use technical terminology when writing about this letter, by asking questions informed by these terms.

With a partner, compare your questions and discuss possible answers to each one. Work together to agree on additional technical terms which could be added to this list, together with the questions that they might help inform.

ACTIVITY

Allow yourself 45 minutes to write a continuation of the student's analysis of Jourdon Anderson's letter, using your notes and ideas. Make sure you address the guiding question, and use technical terms appropriately. In your answer you should make close reference to the letter, and use the quotations that you chose in the previous activity.

Self-assessment

When you have written your analysis, evaluate your work using the criteria for Paper 1. What mark would you give it? What are its strengths? Where and how could it be improved?

OVER TO YOU

This section will have helped you become familiar with the text types that could appear in the guided textual analysis questions in Paper 1. You have read examples of students' plans, responses and essays, and gained a clearer understanding of the assessment criteria.

Make sure you spend some time assessing your own work, and the work of fellow students. Each activity you complete will help you to improve and make progress in this course. The key is to practise regularly, to reflect on where you have improved and to be honest with yourself about where you can still do better.

Paper 2: Comparative essay (SL/HL)

In this section you will:

- learn about the requirements of Paper 2: Comparative essay and how it is assessed
- develop and practise the skills needed to succeed in this paper
- assess examples of responses to comparative essay questions and develop your critical awareness about what the examination requires of you.

Getting started

Start by considering the following points, and making notes on them in your learner portfolio.

- Make a list of all of the texts that you have studied which you might consider using for Paper 2.
- Remember that you cannot use a text for Paper 2 that you have already been assessed on (for instance in the IO or the HL essay).
- Your teacher may have suggested texts which would work well for Paper 2.
- Decide which two or three texts you think will work best in this paper. They should be texts that you know very well, that you can make connections between and that you will be able to write about convincingly from memory.
- What similarities and differences are there between each of the literary works you have chosen?

Outline of assessment and task

Here are the key features of Paper 2:

- You will take this paper at the end of your course.
- You are allowed 1 hour 45 minutes for this exam.
- You will be asked to write a comparative essay on *two* literary texts that you haven't used for the IO or the HL essay.
- You will choose *one* question from four available options which you will not have seen before.
- You will not be allowed to take your texts with you into the examination, so you will need to learn quotations in preparation for this paper.
- Paper 2 is worth 25% of the overall mark at HL and 35% at SL.

For both HL and SL there are four assessment criteria for Paper 2:

Criterion A	Knowledge, understanding and interpretation	10 marks
Criterion B	Analysis and evaluation	10 marks
Criterion C	Focus and organisation	5 marks
Criterion D	Language	5 marks
Total		**30 marks**

Each of these criteria has grade descriptors to aid students, teachers and examiners evaluate the quality of your work. You should familiarise yourself with them so that you know how you are being assessed, and how you may need to improve your work in order to move up to a higher grade band.

Here are the four criteria with the key words and phrases.

Criterion A: Knowledge, understanding and interpretation

Marks	Level descriptor
0	Does not reach the standard required.
1–2	**Little** knowledge or understanding; **little** meaningful comparison of the works.
3–4	**Some** knowledge or understanding of the works; only a **superficial** attempt to compare.
5–6	**Satisfactory** knowledge, understanding and interpretation of the works.
7–8	**Good** knowledge and understanding; **sustained** interpretation of implications and **convincing** interpretation of similarities and differences.
9–10	**Perceptive** knowledge and understanding; **persuasive** interpretation of implications and **insightful** interpretation of similarities and differences.

Criterion B: Analysis and evaluation

Marks	Level descriptor
0	Does not reach the standard required.
1–2	The essay is **descriptive** and offers **little** relevant analysis of textual features.
3–4	Some **appropriate** analysis; mostly descriptive; **superficial** comparisons between the works.
5–6	**Generally appropriate** analysis and **adequate** comparison of works.
7–8	**Appropriate** and **at times insightful** analysis; **good** evaluation and comparison of works.
9–10	**Consistently insightful** and **convincing** analysis; **very good** evaluation and comparison of works.

Criterion C: Focus and organisation

Marks	Level descriptor
0	Does not reach the standard required.
1	**Rare** focus and **few** connections.
2	**Some** focus and connections but **unbalanced**.
3	**Maintains** focus, **mostly balanced** and **mostly logical**; ideas **generally** connected.
4	**Mostly clear and sustained** focus; **balanced** and **logical**; ideas **cohesively** connected.
5	**Clear and sustained** focus; **well balanced**, logical and **convincing**; ideas **cogently** connected.

Criterion D: Language

Marks	Level descriptor
0	Does not reach the standard required.
1	Language is **rarely** clear; there are **many** errors.
2	Language is **sometimes** clear; grammar, vocabulary and sentence construction are **fairly accurate**; register and style are **sometimes appropriate**.
3	Language is **clear** and **carefully chosen**; grammar, vocabulary and sentence construction are **adequately accurate**; register and style are **mostly appropriate**.
4	Language is **clear** and **carefully chosen**; **good degree of accuracy** in grammar, vocabulary and sentence construction; register and style are **consistently appropriate**.
5	Language is **very clear, effective, precise** and **carefully chosen**; **high degree of accuracy** in grammar, vocabulary and sentence construction; register and style are **effective** and **appropriate**.

Preparing your texts for Paper 2

In preparation for the Paper 2 exam, you will need to learn as many carefully selected quotations as possible. Developing a strategy to organise the quotations you have learnt will help you use them most effectively to answer your chosen question.

- Write down as many generic themes as you can that might link your texts (for example, gender representation and relations; politics; appearance and reality).

- For each of these themes, list five quotations from each of your texts in order to start thinking about how you can organise your existing knowledge.

- Keep in mind that the most important thing you should do in the exam is to *answer the question*.

- Organise this information into a revision grid, using themes that are relevant to your particular texts. The following example uses *Macbeth* and *To Kill a Mockingbird* (two works you might have read previously) as examples. You should complete a similar grid for your own texts.

Identity

In the literature you have read, you will have noticed how characters are constantly trying to make sense of who they are and how other people perceive them. Sometimes characters present false identities (like Macbeth, in this example); sometimes they struggle to forge a consistent identity. As you read this chapter, consider what strategies writers use for presenting characters' identities.

TIP

When revising for Paper 2, as well as learning quotations you should look back at previous Paper 2 questions and use these to plan essays as part of your revision.

Text	Appearance and reality	Politics	Individuals and society	Gender representation
Macbeth	'Your face, my thane, is as a book where men may read strange matters'	'He was a gentleman on whom I built/ An absolute trust'	'a poor player/ That struts and frets his hour upon the stage/ And then is heard no more'	'unsex me here,/ And fill me from the crown to the toe topful/ Of direst cruelty!'
To Kill a Mockingbird	'Boo was about six-and-a-half feet tall, judging from his tracks'	'Our courts have our faults, as does any human institution, but in this country our courts are the great levelers, and in our courts all men are created equal.'	'I think there's just one kind of folks. Folks.'	'I was not so sure, but Jem told me I was being a girl, that girls always imagined things, that's why other people hated them so ...'

Looking for question setting patterns

Paper 2 contains *four* questions from which you have to choose *one*. Remember that IB examiners need to set questions that will be relevant for students who have studied a range of different literary works. Therefore, the questions will often be quite broad and unspecific. In fact, if you look carefully at past Paper 2 questions, you may be able to see patterns emerging. For example, you might find that there is often a question on the themes of gender or conflict, or on the structure or language of the works. By completing an analysis of past questions, you can make your revision more focused by revising themes that feature within these generic question patterns.

How should you decide which question to answer?

There will always be *four* questions on Paper 2, and you are required to answer only *one*. You should aim to use the 5 minutes' reading time at the start of the exam to decide which question you are going to answer.

Choosing the right question is an important skill. Don't be tempted to choose the one that seems 'easiest' on first reading. You should think about which question will give you the best opportunity to show what you know, make the strongest arguments, and demonstrate your knowledge of a range of quotations from both texts.

Here are two sets of sample questions of the type that you might find on a Paper 2 exam paper.

Set 1

1   How and why might two of the works that you have studied be considered life-changing?

2   How and to what purpose do the writers of two works you have studied use the natural and built environment in their writing?

3   How and to what purpose do two of the works you have studied explore the tensions between appearance and reality?

4   How and to what purpose do two of the works you have studied explore difficult human relationships?

Set 2

1   How and to what purpose do two of the works you have studied explore the tensions between an individual and society?

2   How and in what ways are contexts important to your understanding of two of the works you have studied?

3   Sometimes works are considered to have an important moral or ethical dimension. Discuss how moral or ethical issues are explored in two of the works you have studied.

4   Many works have one or more important turning points. Discuss how turning points are explored in two of the works you have studied.

ACTIVITY

Look at the two sets of sample Paper 2 question types.

- Think about your two chosen texts.

- Take about 5 minutes to decide which question you would choose from each set, and why.

- Later, you might want to use these questions when you are writing or planning practice essays as part of your revision.

Writing an introductory paragraph

TIP

To write an effective introductory paragraph, make sure that your introduction makes a really clear, focused argument, and very clearly shows *how* you will answer the question.

The first thing that many students will write in the Paper 2 examination is the introduction to their essay. A good introduction starts the essay in a focused and convincing manner, and shows the examiner how you are going to answer the question and how you will compare the two texts. For your introduction, you should aim to:

- write *one* concise paragraph, consisting of three to six sentences

- use the language of the question

- mention both of your literary works, and their authors

- include a final 'thesis statement' which shows *how* you will answer the question and *how* you will make comparisons between the two works.

Sample introductory paragraph

Here is an introductory paragraph written by a student, Lucas, who has decided to answer the following, from the list of sample questions:

How and to what purpose do two of the works you have studied explore difficult human relationships?

He has decided to write about Arthur Miller's play *Death of a Salesman* and F. Scott Fitzgerald's novel *The Great Gatsby*. His response has been annotated to show how he has structured his introductory paragraph.

2

This is a concise paragraph of five sentences

It clearly highlights the two works, and their authors, that the student will be using to answer the question

Arthur Miller's 'Death of a Salesman' presents the audience with Willy Loman's deeply problematic relationships with his sons. Because he lives in the past in his head, he is condemned to hanging onto only an 'air of the dream' of fulfilled family relationships. The same is true in F. Scott Fitzgerald's 'The Great Gatsby' where Gatsby similarly fails to make his dreams a reality. His relationships with Daisy, with Tom, and even with Nick, prove particularly difficult because he cannot repeat the past and so he is always expecting the relationships to be something they cannot be. Gatsby and Loman struggle with human relationships because the images of those relationships that exist in their heads do not match the realities of the worlds they live in.

The introduction uses the language of the question and appropriate synonyms ('deeply problematic relationships'; 'fulfilled family relationships'; 'relationships … prove particularly difficult'; 'struggle with human relationships') in order to be focused on answering the question

The paragraph finished with a final 'thesis statement' which shows how the student will answer the question and how he will make comparisons between the two works

TIP

Practise writing introductions and arguments as a very useful revision strategy. It can help you to start thinking and planning exactly how you will make connections and comparisons between your chosen texts.

ACTIVITY

Have a go at writing an introduction to one of the sample questions, based on two texts that you have studied and that you might use to answer the comparative question in the Paper 2 exam. Remember to make your argument (your 'thesis') as specific and clear as possible in response to the question you have selected.

KEY CONCEPT

Perspective

Death of a Salesman and *The Great Gatsby* are both concerned with equality and inequality and how these are viewed from the perspective of each of the characters. Willy Loman spends his life struggling to make ends meet whereas Gatsby is financially successful and yet fails to be fully accepted into the social world to which he aspires. Despite the centrality of the American Dream in the two works, they both offer a fairly bleak perspective of the possibilities for social mobility in the different parts of American society they present.

Writing body paragraphs and topic sentences

In this section you will work through the process of planning a paragraph in a Paper 2 essay in response to a specific question. You will see how this planning process can be broken down into stages. You will then have the opportunity to try writing your own paragraphs before reading and assessing a whole Paper 2 essay.

Over the next few pages, you will look at the steps followed by a student, Sophia, in planning a response to a Paper 2-style comparative essay question. Sophia has been studying two poetry texts: *Selected Poems* by the 19th-century American poet Emily Dickinson, and *The World's Wife* by the contemporary Scottish poet Carol Ann Duffy.

In the exercise that follows, Sophia is planning a comparative paragraph for an essay in response to the following question:

How and in what ways do two works that you have studied explore what some writers have considered the fragility of human existence?

When you start making connections between your two texts, it is important that you select material from those texts carefully and sensibly. In this worked example, Sophia has chosen two poems from the collections she is studying, which she will use in this particular paragraph.

ACTIVITY

Read the two poems: 'Because I could not stop for Death' by Emily Dickinson and 'Mrs Lazarus' by Carol Ann Duffy. As you read them, annotate the poems and use the annotations to help you understand them better.

Writing a body paragraph

Each time you plan a paragraph you will need to consider very carefully:

- how it will help you to answer the question
- how it fits in with your overall thesis
- what the specific focus of the paragraph will be.

ACTIVITY

When you have read the two poems, you should be able to start thinking about how your ideas could be organised to help you answer the question 'How and in what ways do two works that you have studied explore what some writers have considered the fragility of human existence?'.

Working with another student, plan a paragraph which would answer this question. Follow these steps:

- Draft a topic sentence.
- Pick out the quotations you would use.
- Discuss what you would say about those quotations.

Writing effective topic sentences

As you plan a paragraph and think about writing the first–or 'topic'–sentence of that paragraph, here are some questions that you should be asking yourself:

- Are you giving your reader a sense of precisely what the paragraph will be about and, if appropriate, directing your reader to the relevant extract(s) or element(s) of your text?
- Are you linking back to your thesis?
- Are you answering the question?

TIP

Writing well-focused, organised answers

Focus and organisation are assessed in Criteria C. A focused and organised answer should have:

- a clearly argued introduction which shows how you will answer the question

- carefully focused topic sentences at the start of each body paragraph which help to support a focus which is clear and sustained

- developed ideas that are connected in a logical and convincing manner.

- Are you using a keyword from the question or thesis (or a synonym of that keyword)?
- If you read the first sentence of each of your paragraphs one after another, does this read as a summary of your overall argument?

Self and peer-assessment

Have a go at writing a topic sentence to compare the Dickinson and Duffy texts. Then, either on your own, or swapping your sentence with a partner, check it carefully against all of these bullet points. Have you managed to answer all of those questions in your sentence?

Sample topic sentence

After considering the guidance for writing effective topic sentences, Sophia has decided to focus her paragraph on the poets' attitudes to death in these two poems. Read the topic sentence she has drafted, which has been annotated to help you understand the decisions she is making with her planning and writing.

> The student starts by drawing attention to the texts she will use in this paragraph, and their authors

> Here a direct reference to the essay question ensures she is focused on answering the question

In Dickinson's 'Because I could not stop for Death' and Duffy's 'Mrs Lazarus', the poets present the fragility of human existence in terms of exploring attitudes to death; for Dickinson human life is presented as temporary and death, therefore, as inevitable, whereas for Duffy, the idea that life could be reanimated and that death could therefore be cheated, is shocking and unnatural.

> Here the topic sentence becomes more specific and constructs a mini-thesis for the paragraph (it would also be possible to organise this into two sentences)

> The start to this paragraph makes a specific point in relation to each poem and anticipates the argument that the paragraph will develop

ACTIVITY

Decide which two texts you will be using for Paper 2 then have a go at planning a series of paragraphs, starting with writing the topic sentences and using this worked example as a model.

The next step for Sophia is to pick out the most relevant and useful quotations from the poems. This is helpful for your revision, to identify the quotations you will need to learn for use in the exam. Think about how we might select relevant material from those poems in order to help plan and write a comparative essay.

First, read carefully the poem 'Because I could not stop for Death' by Emily Dickinson. The text has been annotated to explain words that might not be familiar to you, and to highlight some areas which you might consider using in a comparative essay in response to the question.

KEY CONCEPT

Creativity

Emily Dickinson's poems are wonderfully creative. In using powerful images and novel ideas, she invites her reader to see the world in new and different ways. As a student of literature, you should aim to identify and write about moments of creativity as unique and sometimes startling ways of seeing the world, and how the texts you read create memorable images and challenging ideas.

Because I could not stop for Death

Emily Dickinson

Because I could not stop for Death –
He kindly stopped for me –
The Carriage held but just Ourselves –
And Immortality.

We slowly drove – He knew no haste
And I had put away
My labor and my leisure too,
For His Civility –

We passed the School, where Children strove
At Recess – in the Ring –
We passed the Fields of Gazing Grain –
We passed the Setting Sun –

Or rather – He passed Us –
The Dews drew quivering and Chill –
For only Gossamer, my Gown –
My Tippet – only Tulle –

We paused before a House that seemed
A Swelling of the Ground –
The Roof was scarcely visible –
The Cornice – in the Ground –

Since then – 'tis Centuries – and yet
Feels shorter than the Day
I first surmised the Horses' Heads
Were toward Eternity –

Death is represented metaphorically as a coachman, taking the narrator and the reader on a preternatural journey beyond life

The poem suggests that death is under no pressure to act quickly: death is inevitable and universal

This stanza could be read as a metaphor for the passing of life from childhood, to the prime of life, to the end of days (represented by the 'Setting Sun', as the day, or life, comes to an end)

The poem registers a shiver of realisation ('quivering and Chill' that death will come to everyone eventually

'Gossamer' is something very fine or delicate

A 'tippet' is a scarf or shawl

'Tulle' is a material like silk or cotton

In the extended metaphor of the poem, the 'House' might represent a grave

A 'Cornice' is a part of a wall or ceiling which goes around the top of a room

This is a poem which takes the reader on a journey outside time and explores the place of individual human existence in the context of 'eternity' – of all time

The horses pulling the coachman, Death's, carriage are pointing 'toward Eternity' because their journey has one inevitable and unavoidable conclusion

2

KEY CONCEPT

Representation

Much of the literature that you will study in your course explores how human beings try to come to terms with the inevitability of their own death and how death is represented in various different social, cultural and religious contexts.

Coming to terms with death can offer a sense of peace and consolation. Do you think that the poem 'Because I could not stop for Death', or other works that you have read, provide such a sense of hope and reassurance? How do you think this poem represents the idea of death?

Let's now consider the quotations we might want to select as we plan our body paragraph. Look back and remind yourself of the sample topic sentence. Remember that the focus of our paragraph is going to be attitudes to death, and particularly how 'human life is presented as temporary and death, therefore, as inevitable'.

ACTIVITY

Pick out four or five quotations from the poem 'Because I could not stop for Death' that you think would be most useful to answer the question 'How and in what ways do two works that you have studied explore what some writers have considered the fragility of human existence?'. Then think carefully about why you chose these quotations and how you would write about them in an essay. Discuss your ideas with another student.

Sophia has chosen the following quotations as the most helpful in terms of answering the question. She has written them in her revision notes to learn in advance of the exam.

- 'We passed the Fields of Gazing Grain –/ We passed the Setting Sun –'
- 'The Dews drew quivering and Chill'
- 'Since then – 'tis Centuries – and yet/ Feels shorter than the Day'
- 'the Horses' Heads/ Were toward Eternity –'

TIP

Using flashcards for revision

When you are revising for Paper 2, one of the key things that you will need to do is to learn quotations. The more you can learn, the better. One very good strategy for learning quotations is to write each of them out on a flashcard with a prompt or a theme on the other side.

ACTIVITY

Using flashcards to learn quotations

- Start making your own revision flashcards as explained in the Tip feature. Once you have made a few, you can start to test yourself.
- If you definitely know a quotation, put that flashcard on one pile.
- Make another pile for the quotations you still need to learn.

When revising, make sure you always start again with the quotations you *didn't* know the time before. This is an excellent way to revise.

Using flashcards to plan essays

Once you've completed a set of flashcards with your chosen quotations, you can use them to plan your revision essays. This is another excellent way to revise.

- Choose an essay question.
- Pick out all the quotations that you will use as evidence for answering this question.
- Put the cards into the order in which you will use them, and change the order to make the strongest possible argument.
- Remember that your quotations are the evidence that is the backbone of your argument!

Writing effective analytical body paragraphs

Here is a series of questions that you should ask yourself, to check that you are writing effective analytical paragraphs in the body of your essay.

- Have you included several sentences specifically analysing the quotation you have used ('taking apart and demonstrating to us how it works')?

- Have you used technical language and demonstrated that you understand how that technique operates?

- Have you used technical language consistently? For example, are you labelling words as 'adjective', 'verb', etc.?

- Have you avoided describing or paraphrasing (have you avoided 'showing')?

- Have you analysed the effects of the writer's choices of language, form and structure while thinking of the text as a construct?

- Is your analysis helping you to answer the question?

Self- and peer-assessment

Now have a go at writing your own analytical paragraph for 'Because I could not stop for Death'. You should use the plan you created in the activity you did just before the poem, and the relevant quotations which you have selected.

When you have written your paragraph, assess your work using the Tips and guidance in this section. You can either assess your own work or swap with a partner to peer-assess each other's paragraphs. You should refer to the top-level descriptors for each criterion, given in the following table. Where might you need to improve? Aim to bring your work as close to this top-level standard as possible.

Criterion A: Knowledge, understanding and interpretation	**Perceptive** knowledge and understanding; **persuasive** interpretations of implications, and **insightful** interpretations of similarities and differences.
Criterion B: Analysis and evaluation	**Consistently insightful** and **convincing** analysis and **very good** evaluation and comparison of works.
Criterion C: Focus and organisation	**Clear and sustained** focus; **well balanced, logical** and **convincing**; ideas **cogently** connected.
Criterion D: Language	Language is **very clear, effective, precise** and **carefully chosen; high degree of accuracy** in grammar, vocabulary and sentence construction; register and style are **effective** and **appropriate**.

Decide what you think you've done well and which areas you could improve on. Once you've done this, redraft your paragraph before reading the next example.

Having drafted a topic sentence and selected the quotations for the first section of her paragraph, Sophia has written the next part of the paragraph, following the guidance given in this section on writing good analytical paragraphs.

As you read, pay careful attention to the way in which Sophia has included the quotations from the poem that she chose when she was planning her paragraph. Her response has been annotated to show how she has structured her paragraph and her argument.

The section starts by giving a very succinct overview of the structuring metaphor of the poem as a whole

Here the student focuses on how specifically metaphor is used in order to represent life and impending death in the poem

By zooming in on the specific details, the student is able to identify some of the ways in which the poet uses imagery and figurative language

The argument of this section of the paragraph is re-focused on its overall thesis

Dickinson's poem takes as its structuring metaphor the idea of death as a carriage driver taking the narrator on a journey; in that journey of life the 'Fields of Gazing Grain' might represent the prime of life (with the alliterative 'Gazing Grain' suggesting the vitality of existence) and the 'Setting Sun' metaphorically representing the end of life. The movement towards ending is registered with a distinct change of mood when 'The Dews drew quivering and Chill'. The fragile human body shivers ('quivering' is functionally onomatopoeic) and feels the 'Chill' cold. This momentary realisation triggers a perspective shift, where 'Centuries' have passed (Death has taken the narrator and reader on a journey beyond death and time) which nevertheless 'Feels shorter than the Day' because the poet realises the inevitability of the 'Horses' Heads' pointing 'toward Eternity': human life is presented as temporary and death, therefore, as unavoidable.

Now, in comparison, read the poem 'Mrs Lazarus' by Carol Ann Duffy. In the Gospel of St John from the Christian Bible, Lazarus is a man who is ill but dies before Jesus has the chance to heal him. When Jesus does arrive in his town, Lazarus has already been laid in his tomb. Jesus asks for the stone in front of the tomb to be rolled away, and he calls to Lazarus to come out. Lazarus walks out still dressed in his death-clothes and is brought back to life. In the story of this miracle, Jesus resurrects Lazarus from the dead. Carol Ann Duffy's poem tells this story from the point of view of Lazarus's wife. The poem has been annotated for you, to highlight some of its key features and unfamiliar words.

Mrs Lazarus

Carol Ann Duffy

I had grieved. I had wept for a night and a day
over my loss, ripped the cloth I was married in
from my breasts, howled, shrieked, clawed
at the burial stones until my hands bled, retched
his name over and over again, dead, dead.

Gone home. Gutted the place. Slept in a single cot,
widow, one empty glove, white femur
in the dust, half. Stuffed dark suits
into black bags, shuffled in a dead man's shoes,
noosed the double knot of a tie around my bare neck,

gaunt nun in the mirror, touching herself. I learnt
the Stations of Bereavement, the icon of my face
in each bleak frame; but all those months
he was going away from me, dwindling
to the shrunk size of a snapshot, going,

The poem opens with a conventional representation (if rather melodramatic, which might make us slightly suspicious) of the grief of a wife for her dead husband

A 'femur' is a thighbone

'Stations of Bereavement' is a reference to the 'Stations of the Cross' and describes various stages of grief (in the Catholic Church, each of the 14 Stations of the Cross represents an event from Jesus's last day, from his condemnation to his execution, and a separate prayer is said for each stage of his suffering)

going. Till his name was no longer a certain spell

for his face. The last hair on his head

floated out from a book. His scent went from the house.

The will was read. See, he was vanishing

to the small zero held by the gold of my ring.

Then he was gone. Then he was legend, language;

my arm on the arm of the schoolteacher – the shock

of a man's strength under the sleeve of his coat –

along the hedgerows. But I was faithful

for as long as it took. Until he was <u>memory</u>.

So I could stand that evening in the field

in a shawl of fine air, healed, able

to watch the edge of the moon occur to the sky

and a hare thump from a hedge; then notice

the village men running towards me, <u>shouting,</u>

behind them the women and children, barking dogs,

and I knew. I knew by the sly light

on the blacksmith's face, the shrill eyes

of the barmaid, the sudden hands bearing me

into the hot tang of the crowd parting <u>before me.</u>

He lived. I saw the horror on his face.

I heard his mother's crazy song. I breathed

his stench; my bridegroom in his rotting shroud,

moist and dishevelled from the grave's slack chew,

croaking his cuckold name, disinherited, <u>out</u> of <u>his time.</u>

This stanza presents the way in which deceased people become memories as the time since their death increases

This stanza registers a kind of hiatus before the news breaks and a new reality (the resurrection of her husband) has to be confronted

Sights, sounds and smells are vividly foregrounded as the narrator realises what's happened

This stanza is full of unpleasant sensations from the full range of the senses and creates a kind of haunting experience

KEY CONCEPT

Transformation

Notice how often literature focuses on the way in which behaviours and attitudes are transformed by particular events. Things that take place on a national or even international level can transform our behaviours and attitudes. At other moments, those events may be more personal, even domestic, as in this poem.

Just as she did for the first poem, Sophia now decided which quotations she would use in order to conclude her paragraph. She focused on how the idea that life could be reanimated and that death could be cheated is shocking and unnatural. She decided to focus on the following quotations and added these to her revision notes:

- 'howled, shrieked, clawed/ at the burial stones until my hands bled, retched/ his name over and over again'

- 'Then he was gone. Then he was legend, language'

- 'He lived. I saw the horror on his face./ I heard his mother's crazy song. I breathed/ his stench'.

Sample analytical paragraph

Sophia used her notes to write the following analytical paragraph on 'Mrs Lazarus'. Read the paragraph and the annotations carefully, paying particular attention to the structure and the way she has used quotations as evidence.

The section starts by giving a very succinct overview of the poem and by referencing (as concisely as possible) the key bits of context which are necessary to understand the poem's argument

Here the student focuses on how specifically a range of literary techniques are being used in order to present the emotions of the central figure in the poem

Note how she 'zooms' in on specific details to focus on particular examples and language

> In comparison, Duffy's poem is written from the perspective of Lazarus's wife who experiences death and then is forced to confront her dead husband having being brought back from the tomb. In the Bible story which is her source material, Lazarus's dead body is reanimated by Jesus a couple of days after his death. Before this happens, however, Lazarus's wife experiences the full range of grief. The poem describes how she 'howled, shrieked, clawed/ at the burial stones until my hands bled, retched/ his name over and over again'. The onomatopoeic triad of physical verbs ('howled, shrieked, clawed'), the visceral 'retched' - suggesting her being literally sick - and the desperate repetition ('over and over again') all suggest the brutal reality of her grief and of the pain of confronting death. However, as her husband is transfigured into memory - 'Then he was legend, language' - we begin to realise that Mrs Lazarus is not quite as disappointed as her actions first suggested. In fact, her response is to recognise the fragility of human life for what it is and to move on; soon, we see, she is 'healed' and able to renew her life and relationships. This poem, however, has one terrible final shock in store when, following the miracle, Mrs Lazarus realises that, once again: 'He lived.' At this point she tells us how: 'I saw the horror on his face./ I heard his mother's crazy song. I breathed/ his stench' and the repugnant sensual responses ('horror'; 'crazy song'; 'stench') register the horrific and shocking unnaturalness of death being cheated.

The paragraph now traces the way in which the poem's narrative steers away from the initial grief and towards a process of moving on

In the final section of the paragraph, the student looks at the poem's concluding stanza and explores how the ideas here fit into her overall argument and paragraph thesis

We have now examined these two poems and explored the ways in which we might use material from them in planning a Paper 2 response. Let's now think about how that whole paragraph might look. Remember that Paper 2 asks you to write a *comparative* essay. You should, therefore, always be looking for connections and points of comparison between the two texts. In making these connections, you may find it helpful to use some of the linking words and phrases suggested in the Tip feature that follows the sample paragraph.

Sample comparative paragraph

Here is a sample paragraph, written by Sophia, which compares the two poems. Read this paragraph carefully, thinking about the ways in which it is structured and uses quotations from the text, before completing the exercise which follows it.

In Dickinson's 'Because I could not stop for Death' and Duffy's 'Mrs Lazarus', the poets present the fragility of human existence in terms of exploring attitudes to death; for Dickinson human life is presented as temporary and death, therefore, as inevitable whereas, for Duffy, the idea that life could be reanimated and that death could, therefore, be cheated is shocking and unnatural. Dickinson's poem takes as its structuring metaphor the idea of death as a carriage driver taking the narrator on a journey; in that journey of life the 'Fields of Gazing Grain' might represent the prime of life (with the alliterative 'Gazing Grain' suggesting the vitality of existence) and the 'Setting Sun' metaphorically representing the end of life. The movement towards ending is registered with a distinction change of mood when: 'The Dews drew quivering and Chill'. The fragile human body shivers ('quivering' is functionally onomatopoeic) and feels the 'Chill' cold. This momentary realisation triggers a perspective shift where 'Centuries' have passed (Death has taken the narrator and reader on a journey beyond death and time) which nevertheless 'Feels shorter than the Day' because the poem realises the inevitability of the 'Horses' Heads' pointing 'toward Eternity': human life is presented as temporary and death, therefore, as unavoidable. In comparison, Duffy's poem is written from the perspective of Lazarus's wife who experiences death and then is forced to confront her dead husband having being brought back from the tomb. In the Bible story which is her source material, Lazarus's dead body is reanimated by Jesus a couple of days after his death. Before this happens, however, Lazarus's wife experiences the full range of grief. The poem describes how she 'howled, shrieked, clawed/ at the burial stones until my hands bled, retched/ his name over and over again'. The onomatopoeic triad of physical verbs ('howled, shrieked, clawed'), the visceral 'retched' - suggesting her being literally sick - and the desperate repetition ('over and over again') all suggest the brutal reality of her grief and of the pain of confronting death. However, as her husband is transfigured into memory - 'Then he was legend, language' - we begin to realise that Mrs Lazarus is not quite as disappointed as her actions first suggested. In fact, her response is to recognise the fragility of human life for what it is and to move on; soon, we see, she is 'healed' and able to renew her life and relationships. This poem, however, has one terrible final shock in store when, following the miracle, Mrs Lazarus realises that, once again: 'He lived.' At this point she tells us how: 'I saw the horror on his face./ I heard his mother's crazy song. I breathed/ his stench' and the repugnant sensual responses ('horror'; 'crazy song'; 'stench') register the horrific and shocking unnaturalness of death being cheated.

ACTIVITY

After you have read the sample response, return to the paragraph you wrote and redrafted earlier, or write another paragraph based on your own choice of Paper 2 texts. Develop your paragraph using the following bullet points as prompts. Write at least *one* sentence which develops each of these ideas. This will help you to develop effective analytical and evaluation skills.

- Have you considered how contexts of both reception (when the text was read or watched) and production (when the text was written) might inform your reading?

- Have you considered how and why these contexts might be important?

- Have you considered different possible interpretations, critical interpretations and perspectives?

- Have you used a formula such as 'on the one hand … on the other hand …' to explore different possible interpretations?

TIP
You might find the following phrases helpful when comparing and contrasting your texts:

Differences
on the other hand
however
alternatively
conversely
in contrast
in comparison

Similarities
in a similar vein
in the same way
equally

You might find the following phrases helpful when writing about cause and effect:

therefore
this suggests
as a consequence
in this way
for this reason
in this vein
this registers

ACTIVITY (CONTINUED)

- Have you quoted a critic? If so, is the quotation concise and specific? Have you evaluated whether or not you agree and why?
- Have you finished the paragraph by focusing on the question?
- Are you making effective connections?

KEY CONCEPT
Communication

In writing about marriage, Duffy is communicating powerful ways of thinking about such a relationship. The clarity of that communication is key. In your writing, you need to communicate your ideas and arguments as concisely and precisely as possible, in order to communicate effectively and clearly to your reader.

ACTIVITY

Using the phrases in the Tip feature, practise writing ten sentences that link your own two or three texts in any ways that you think are interesting. Aim to use as many of the linking words and phrases as possible, and to think about cause and effect.

Self-assessment

Having worked through the process of preparing, planning and writing a comparative essay body paragraph, now read your own paragraph again to yourself very carefully. As you read, check that you have followed the guidance you have been given throughout this section.

Think about how you can ensure that you apply this guidance to your own comparative essays throughout this course.

REFLECT
Before you look at an example of a full student response to the question, take some time to remind yourself what you have learnt so far in this section. Make brief notes to consider what you will need to remember about:

- the assessment criteria for Paper 2
- the function of an introduction
- writing effective topic sentences
- developing analytical and evaluative body paragraphs.

Which two or three texts have you decided to prepare for your Paper 2 examination? Choose one of the sample Paper 2-style questions at the beginning of this section, and have a go at preparing, planning and writing your own comparative essay body paragraph, using your chosen texts. Follow the same step-by-step process that you have worked through in this section. You should write *one* developed paragraph which starts with a clear topic sentence, and use evidence from your chosen texts to support your points.

Peer-assessment

Once you have finished writing a paragraph using your own chosen texts, swap your work with a fellow student.

- Have they addressed all of the assessment criteria (see the following table for a reminder of the criteria and what is needed for the top band)?

- Have they made effective use of the suggested approaches and strategies in this section (now would be an good opportunity to go back and make sure you've remembered these!)? Use this table to remind yourself what qualities the examiners are looking for in order to achieve the top band.

Criterion A	Knowledge, understanding and interpretation	Your knowledge and understanding should be **perceptive**, your response to the question should be **persuasive**, and your interpretation of the connections between the two texts should be **insightful**.	10 marks
Criterion B	Analysis and evaluation	Your analysis of the text features and writers' choices should be **consistently insightful**. Your evaluation of how those choices shape the meaning of the text should be **very good**.	10 marks
Criterion C	Focus and organisation	Your focus should be **clear, sustained, and well balanced**. Your ideas should be **logical and convincing**.	5 marks
Criterion D	Language	Your language and writing style should be very **accurate, clear and effective**. The register of your writing should be **appropriate to the task**.	5 marks
Total			**30 marks**

Sample full student essay

You will now examine a full student response to a comparative essay question. This sample essay has been annotated to highlight its key features, and to help you think about how it is addressing the assessment criteria.

The essay compares the play *King Lear* by William Shakespeare and the novel *Things Fall Apart* by Chinua Achebe. It answers one of the sample Paper 2-style questions from the start of this section:

How and to what purpose do two of the works you have studied explore the tensions between appearance and reality?

KEY CONCEPT

Cultural attitudes to mental health

You will notice that both of the 'tragic heroes' compared in this essay struggle with their mental health, at least in today's terms. How useful do you think it is to apply your contemporary understanding of issues around mental health to times and cultures which might have viewed these issues in very different ways?

The introduction starts with a brief overview of the essay question in relation to both works, addressing Criterion A through demonstration of understanding.

The introduction compares and contrasts the two texts, organising and focusing its argument and therefore addressing Criterion C.

The introduction ends with a topic sentence which addresses Criterion C in terms of providing a focus for the essay. Perhaps this introduction could be slightly more concise and precise?

This is a clearly organised topic sentence which provides a focus for the paragraph (Criterion C). It is perhaps rather long: could the student have used two sentences to make this point or employed more concise and precise language?

Okonkwo, the protagonist of 'Things Fall Apart', is presented as a powerful and fearless warrior, and yet the narrator constantly reveals his deep insecurities. He appears to be in control of his situation and surroundings; however, following his complete loss of influence, he ultimately ends his life by committing suicide, disproving this assumption. King Lear, in the same vein, is 'every inch a king': a powerful, ruthless monarch who is autocratic and in control. And yet, in giving away his kingdom to his two scheming daughters, he tears down the façade of his power to reveal a 'weak and despised' old man underneath the trappings of a king. 'Things Fall Apart' exploits its ambiguously biased, omniscient narrator to extend the reader's sympathy for Okonkwo as a compromised and troubled human being; 'King Lear', on the other hand, employs a dense network of imagery around sight and blindness in order to foreground the tensions between what appears to be and what really is. This multidimensional interpretation of the characters' psyche is a central theme in both works. In two contrasting worlds where good and evil are contrasted with each other, Shakespeare and Achebe exploit the complex relationships between appearance and reality to highlight the intricate nature of navigating relationships, and experiences.

The tension between appearance and reality is predominantly registered through the tragic heroes of both works, who are initially presented as successful, strong, and conventionally masculine, yet are ultimately revealed to be psychologically fatally flawed in that they act in a rash and impetuous manner and are not able to respond in socially and conventionally expected ways because of personal emotional constraints. In 'Things Fall Apart', for instance, Okonkwo, whose presence evokes 'perpetual fear' in those around him, presents himself as a man who is impervious to emotions. The narrative, in one of its typical moments of silently endorsing the cultural practices of the Igbo people, affirms that: 'To show affection was a sign of weakness; the only thing worth demonstrating was strength.' The confident, assured tone of the narrative here suggests an unchallengeable ethical position, one that is not susceptible to doubt. Nonetheless, the apparent surface of the implacable Okonkwo is undercut by the very same narrator. At the moment of Ikemefuna's death, the narrator describes how: 'Okonkwo drew his matchet and cut him down. He was afraid of being thought weak.' The two sentences provide an interesting comparison. The opening statement of action is contrasted with the secondary revelation of emotional doubt. The narrative clarity of 'He was afraid' is a revelation in direct contrast to the appearance that Okonkwo has been keen to develop throughout the novel. In a similar vein, despite complaining about his son's 'woman-like' manners, the narrator tells us that 'Okonkwo was inwardly pleased at his son's development'. The adverb ('inwardly') captures an inward life whose reality is captured in the narrative's later, more candid: 'his whole life was dominated by fear, the fear of failure and weakness … the fear of the forest … the fear of himself, lest he should resemble his father.' That haunting repetition of the word 'fear' brings us back to the central psychological trauma of Okonkwo's life: the relationship with his father. In a similar vein, Lear carries an air of authority at the beginning of the play which is diminished as a result of his rash transgressions and narcissistic motivations, ultimately reducing him to a powerless and manipulated man. Lear's arrival is announced by the statement: 'The King is coming'. This conveys respect and esteem and the intimidating tone and warning effectively portray his authoritative image in the initial scenes of the play. In contrast, by Act 3, Lear's self-referential description presents him as a 'poor, infirm, weak and despised old man'. The pejorative series of adjectives are in stark contrast to his previous status and harshly depict his true and transformed qualities.

The tensions between appearance and reality are presented through Shakespeare's and Achebe's respective presentations of the protagonists, particularly in their effect on the audience and readers of the works. However, the images created of Lear and Okonkwo, which are based on their interactions with other characters, their own actions, and the way in which they are perceived, ultimately evoke sympathy. For instance, a sympathetic sentiment is conjured from the audience for Lear when the Fool denounces the loss of 'all thy other titles' and the rashness of the decision to 'give away' all the things which essentially constitute the monarch's power. In the same mode, the reader can witness the manner in which the novel cultivates a sense of compassion for Okonkwo through the loss of his previous potential to acquire 'the Idemili title, the third highest in the land.' However, in the passage leading up to Ikemefuna's brutal murder, the ostensibly third person narrator temporarily slips into the mind of the boy who imagines uniting with his mother and '[sings a song] it in his mind, and [walks] to its beat' as it calms him to think of his past. In doing this, the author is employing free indirect discourse to create an empathic bond between the reader and the character while also registering the extent of Okonkwo's cold cruelty. Furthermore, Okonkwo's cruel and antagonistic identity is accentuated through the brutal attempts to emasculate and 'correct' his son, Nwoye, through 'constant nagging and beating'. In the same way, Goneril and Regan's schemes are a clever use of dramatic irony that allow the audience to sympathize with Lear, portaying the daughters as antagonists and the 'old man' as the victim. They exclaim: 'Pray you let us hit together.'

Knowledge and understanding (Criterion A) are demonstrated through specific examples and accurate and appropriate use of quotations as evidence.

Here the argument offers a convincing analysis of some of the structures of the texts, clearly addressing Criterion B.

By zooming in on the language and analysing and evaluating its effects, the essay continues to address Criterion B.

In comparing the two texts, the essay is demonstrating a clear focus on answering the question and is addressing Criterion C.

There is perhaps more to say about the material from 'King Lear' here; however, the paragraph is already quite long.

This topic sentence is a little repetitive and vague. This could be redrafted to make it address Criterion C even more effectively?

Here, the essay could further explain how the effects it discusses are achieved using literary techniques. This would help the student to perform even more successfully in criterion B.

This is a sophisticated way in which to address Criterion B: by looking at the writer's narrative style and techniques.

The student appears to have tagged on the ending to this paragraph and the comparison, as a result, feels a little forced.

As the essay proceeds, it begins to lack the tight focus of the earlier topic sentences. How could this sentence be even more clearly developed to help address the need for focus in Criterion C?

Here, the use of language is highlighted but could the student have used a technical term (simile?) in order to make the explanation and evaluation even more effective?Do you find this point of comparison completely convincing? How could it be made more so?

Here the rhetorical question could be identified and commented on.

Both protagonists gradually change throughout the texts and we can argue that they lose their minds, their intentions becoming disastrous and causing disruption to the lives of those around them. Okonkwo's madness becomes apparent after the murder of the boy who called him 'father', regardless of having been advised against it. At this point in the novel his daunting fear of failure takes hold of him and he kills Ikemefuna to be in control of the way he appears to others, as a strong and fearless leader that will not stop at anything to defend his clan. Nonetheless, his strength is still apparent and that same evening he 'felt like a drunken giant walking with the limbs of a giant mosquito' as the shocking reality comes crashing down on him eventually. The juxtaposing imagery underlines the internal conflict of the protagonist and conveys how morality and justice for the Igbo cannot coexist in the same body, ultimately leaving Okonkwo a shattered man. In a similar vein, Lear's daughters' calculated betrayal of their father and his banishment to a wild heath causes him to question 'Is man no more but this?' His moment of epiphany and philosophical register undermines his previous identity by stripping his title and riches. The monosyllabic words achieve absolute clarity because the simplicity of his communication to her reveals an absolute truth, speaking to our shared humanity. King Lear is driven to madness when he realises that he has torn his family apart, as shown after he was rejected by both Goneril and Regan and during his encounter with Tom, or Edgar. This results in a complete loss of identity when he asks 'Who is it that can tell me who I am?' and 'Is man no more than this?'

The two narratives are eventually revealed as tragedies; however, the masking of what really is and what appears to be is a central catalyst of these tragedies. Throughout the texts, the façade of what appears to be is slowly unravelled before the reader's and audience's eyes culminating in the presentation of the fragility of two torn men who ultimately end up losing their lives, as is the fate of the tragic hero.

Here the student appears to have run out of time to comment effectively on these last couple of quotations.

This conclusion makes an effort to return to the focused argument set out in the introduction; however, we can see how the student – perhaps writing very quickly at the end of the essay – is not able to be as specific as at the beginning of the essay

Peer-assessment

Once you have finished reading this sample essay, you should assess it, using the criteria and what you have learnt in this section. Discuss it with a partner and perhaps your teacher.

- Refer to the assessment criteria for Paper 2 at the beginning of this section.
- Give the essay a mark out of 30 (10 marks each for Criteria A and B, and 5 marks each for Criteria C and D).

What are the strengths and weaknesses of this response? How could it be improved?

OVER TO YOU

Now that you've worked through all the stages of planning and writing a comparative essay, and assessed a full sample student response, it's your turn to have a go. Working with the texts you are preparing for Paper 2, you should aim to use all of the advice in this section to try planning and writing your own essay. You could use one of the sample Paper 2-style questions at the beginning of the section.

Remember, once you've finished writing, to spend some time, either on your own or with another student, assessing your work and asking yourself what you will do differently, and how you could do better.

It is also an excellent idea to swap your essay with a partner and read each other's work carefully, offering kind and constructive advice for improvement, based on the guidance given in this section and your own understanding of the assessment criteria.

Every practice essay is a step towards performing at your very best in the final Paper 2 examination. You won't get everything right first time; the important thing is to learn from the experience of writing and to aim to improve next time.

Higher-level essay

In this section you will:

- remind yourself of the requirements of the HL essay and how it is assessed
- practise the skills needed to succeed in the HL essay
- examine examples of HL essays and develop your critical awareness about what the essay requires of you.

3

Getting started

All HL students are required to write an essay of between 1200 and 1500 words. You can follow a line of enquiry of your own choice in relation to:

- a non-literary text
- a collection of non-literary texts by the same author
- a literary text studied during the course.

Start by writing down the following information in the form of notes:

- the title and author of the text you plan to write about
- the general line of enquiry that you propose to take
- a first draft of a research question
- one or two sentences of a thesis or argument that show how, at this stage, you are intending to answer the question.

During the writing process, you should expect to redraft your question – also referred to as your 'thesis statement' – several times as you work on refining it and as you approach the final draft of your essay. For now, think about how you can make your research question even more specific. In the section that follows, you can see how one student re-focused her question from her initial starting point.

Using the key concepts

Agreeing on a topic can be difficult because of the range of options available. The seven key concepts for the English A: Language and Literature course can help provide additional focus at the planning stage.

Concept	What does it mean?	How can it be applied?
Identity	How does identity develop as we read a text? Do texts change the reader's view of themselves?	When reading a text, you will interact with many different voices, including the author's, the characters' and your own. The interrelationship between the reader and the author is at the heart of understanding how a text can be received.
Culture	How can you gain a deeper understanding of a culture through reading literature?	Literature can explore a culture's values, beliefs and attitudes of the time. The application of this conceptual understanding should prompt discussions about the extent to which a text is a product of its time and place.
Creativity	What does it mean to be creative? Where does inspiration come from?	Analysing the creative act is central to reading and writing. Writing is a creative act, but so too are reading and writing about a text. Exploring different interpretations of a text is intrinsic to developing a mature reading.
Communication	What different forms of communication are there? How effectively can meaning be conveyed? What part might figurative language play?	Communication between writer and reader is, of course, central to a text, but it is never clear and unambiguous. Understanding the complexity of communication is fundamental to making progress in your course: texts can be heavily symbolic, ambiguous and open to different readings.
Perspective	How many different perspectives are there when reading a text? What do we gain from approaching an episode or issue from a number of different perspectives?	A text can have many different perspectives on one or more issues, and they may or may not reflect the views of the author. Texts may not only contain many perspectives; they are also open to a number of different perspectives, including those of the reader, a critic, a teacher and, of course, the author. Learning to evaluate each of these perspectives is an important skill.

(Continued)

Concept	What does it mean?	How can it be applied?
Transformation	How truly transformative can a text be? To what extent are texts changed by other texts, and by the interaction between the reader and the author's words?	Texts can be transformed when greater understanding develops: realising the influence of different artists and genres on a text can force us to reassess what we know about the text and the culture it was created in. Reading is itself a transformative process, and being able to reflect on how it changes us, and our view of the world around us, is essential to how we develop as human beings.
Representation	How accurately can literature represent reality? Can language only ever be a partial or unstable representation of the world around us?	How writers represent themselves through language, and the worlds they imagine, is open to debate and discussion. Establishing whether it connects with the reader's own interpretation of reality is fundamental to how much we empathise with a text.

Outline of assessment and task

Before we look at examples of HL essays, let's first remind ourselves of exactly what the task is and how it is assessed. As an HL student on the English A: Language and Literature course, you will:

- write a 1200–1500-word essay on a literary or non-literary text
- follow the expectations of a formal literary essay, including the use of citations and references
- be externally assessed by an IB examiner and your essay will count for 20% of your final mark.

There are four assessment criteria for the HL essay:

Criterion A	Knowledge, understanding and interpretation	5 marks
Criterion B	Analysis and evaluation	5 marks
Criterion C	Focus, organisation and development	5 marks
Criterion D	Language	5 marks
Total		**20 marks**

In order to understand exactly what you need to do in order to succeed, you should ask the following questions for each of the criteria.

Criterion A	• How well do you demonstrate knowledge and understanding of the work you have chosen for your HL essay?
	• How well do you support your ideas by references to the work?
	• How effectively do you demonstrate a clear interpretation of the elements of the work you have studied and chosen to write about?
Criterion B	How well do you use your own knowledge of the work you have chosen in order to analyse and evaluate its effectiveness?
Criterion C	• How well do you structure and focus your HL essay?
	• How well do you connect and develop ideas in a coherent manner?
Criterion D	How clear, accurate and effective is the language you use?

The HL essay: a suggested approach

This section is divided into two parts. The first focuses on preparation for HL essays on *non-literary* texts; the second focuses on preparation for HL essays on *literary* texts. Both parts are organised around the following five stages:

- Stage 1: preliminary reading and research
- Stage 2: focused reading and research
- Stage 3: establishing your line of enquiry
- Stage 4: planning your HL essay
- Stage 5: writing your HL essay exemplar.

Writing your HL essay on non-literary texts

We will start this section by looking at the experience of one student who decided to write her HL essay on non-literary texts. Leah is studying art history and is interested in the parallels between 19th-century artist Théodore Géricault's work and the images emerging from the crisis following the war in Syria by Russian photographer Sergey Ponomarev. Ponomarev visited the frontline of the migrant crisis to capture the experiences of those leaving the Middle East and Africa for Europe.

Leah began by exploring the story behind Géricault's most famous painting, *The Raft of the Medusa*, which is reproduced here.

TIP

Remember to keep checking the criteria for this essay, and to make sure that you are consciously thinking about these as you write. It can be easy, given the depth of your analysis, to 'drift' away from the subject matter itself, and your main focus.

Stage 1: preliminary reading and research

Leah began by doing some background reading on Géricault's painting. She was interested not only in how it was conceived and painted but also in the story behind it. She wanted to explore the themes of abandonment, isolation and movement, and the key concept of *community*. She was also interested in exploring whether art could adequately convey human emotions in extreme conditions. Beyond this she had no fixed ideas, but that open-mindedness and receptiveness to different ideas can be advantageous at this stage of your planning.

Leah began her research by visiting the following websites:

- The Louvre – the famous art gallery and museum in Paris, where the painting is exhibited.

- Wikipedia – a good starting point for background information and links to other sources.

- Khan Academy – for a short video introduction to the painting.

Leah made notes in her learner portfolio on the story behind the wrecked boat. She felt that the following quote, from the Louvre website, was particularly important, and she underlined the key phrases.

> 'The whole composition is oriented toward this <u>hope</u> in a rightward ascent culminating in a black figure, the figurehead of the boat. The painting stands as a <u>synthetic view</u> of human life <u>abandoned</u> to its <u>fate</u>.'

Other words and phrases she noted from the Louvre website included:

- pallid bodies

- chiaroscuro

- despair and solitude

- romantic inspiration

- 'The goal of painting is to speak to the soul and eyes, not to repel'.

Leah worked quickly on this stage of her preparation because she knew she wanted to write an essay on Sergey Ponomarev's work. She wanted to explore how an artist could represent human despair, as well as hope. Her teacher suggested she read Julian Barnes's analysis of *The Raft of the Medusa* in his book *Keeping an Eye Open: Essays on Art*. Before doing so, Leah read an interview with Barnes, in *The New Yorker*, which was published online. She copied the following passage into her learner portfolio, and annotated it as she wrote it out.

> Flaubert expressed a similar opinion, Barnes notes in the introduction to Keeping an Eye Open. 'Flaubert believed that it was impossible to explain one art form in terms of another, and that great paintings required no words of explanation,' he writes. But Barnes, of course, disagrees: 'It is a rare picture which stuns, or argues, us into silence,' he writes, 'And if one does, it is only a short time before we want to explain and understand the very silence into which we have been plunged.'

Is this true? Do we not 'translate' all visual texts into words in some way?

I agree with this, but is the same true of other visual texts: photography, film, etc.?

Interesting idea: even the silence has to have meaning. The same would go for any blanks on a canvas, or in a photograph. Explore more.

Notice how Leah questions her source material. She takes notes, but sees them as starting points for her own thinking.

Her reading around the painting led her to an essay published in a UK newspaper, *The Guardian*, in 2012, and she copied the following in her learner portfolio. This was important for Leah, as her notes show:

> 'At an early meeting of the Photographic Society of London, established in 1853, one of the members complained that the new technique was "too literal to compete with works of art" because it was unable to "elevate the imagination". This conception of photography as a mechanical recording medium never fully died away.'
>
> - Really interesting. Is photography literal? Does it interpret? Does it reflect the values of the photographer?
> - Can it 'elevate' the imagination? Or does it simply report fact?
> - To what extent is it 'mechanical'? It uses a machine, rather than a pen or brush: is this behind the criticism?
> - Does this view persist of photography being a second-rate art form?
> - Does the fact that a photograph can be re-published endlessly - and each one is as 'original' as the other - matter? You can't do the same with a painting. Does that matter? Poems and novels are also unoriginal in this sense.

Leah read Barnes's essay on the real story behind Géricault's painting and copied the following passage into her learner portfolio. Barnes is writing about the final survivors of the shipwreck who were floating adrift on the raft.

She has underlined key phrases in the final paragraph:

> After a debate in which the most dreadful despair presided, it was agreed among the fifteen healthy persons that their sick comrades must, for the common good of those who might yet survive, be cast into the sea. Three sailors and a soldier, their hearts now hardened by the constant sight of death, performed these repugnant but necessary executions. The healthy were separated from the unhealthy like the clean from the unclean.
>
> After this cruel sacrifice, the last fifteen survivors threw all their arms into the water, reserving only a sabre lest some rope or wood might need cutting. There was sustenance left for six days while they awaited death.

> Then came a <u>small event</u> which each <u>interpreted</u> according to his nature. <u>A white</u>
> <u>butterfly</u>, of a species common in France, appeared over their heads fluttering, and
> <u>settled upon the sail</u>. To some, <u>crazed with hunger</u>, it seemed that even this could
> make a morsel. To others, <u>the ease with which their visitor moved appeared a very</u>
> <u>mockery of those who lay exhausted and almost motionless beneath it</u>. To yet others,
> this simple butterfly was a <u>sign</u>, a messenger from Heaven <u>as white as Noah's dove</u>.
> Even those sceptical ones who declined to recognise a divine instrument knew that
> butterflies travel little distance from the dry land, and were raised by cautious hope.

She then added another passage from the interview with Barnes in *The New Yorker* which is
linked to the passage above. She has underlined some key phrases.

> What is most striking about the essay is Barnes's detailed accounting of
> Géricault's many <u>artistic choices:</u> he considers what Géricault could have chosen
> to paint, what each choice would have implied, and why, finally, Géricault painted
> what he did. The whole thing is shot through with the obvious admiration of <u>one</u>
> <u>artist for the craftsmanship of another</u>. <u>The actual Medusa was famously visited by</u>
> <u>a white butterfly</u>, which Géricault did not include in the painting; had he included
> it, Barnes writes, '<u>it wouldn't look like a true event</u>, even though it was; what is <u>true</u>
> <u>is not necessarily convincing</u>.' Later in the essay, he adds: '<u>Truth to life, at the start</u>
> <u>to be sure; yet once the progress gets under way, truth to art is the greater allegiance</u>.'

REFLECT

Why do you think
that Leah underlined
these phrases? Why
do you think they may
be important, and
where do you think
they could lead in
establishing a line of
enquiry?

Stage 2: focused reading and research

Leah's work on Géricault's painting had raised a lot of questions, but it had also moved her on to
start thinking about the truth of art, and whether all forms of art can be equally 'true'.

Instead of starting her research with a predetermined idea of what she wanted to do, she allowed
her research to lead her. This can often result in the most persuasive and interesting essays because
they are rooted in established and linked ideas.

Next she turned her attention to Sergey Ponomarev's work and in particular looked at this image.

From her preliminary research on Géricault, she had a number of questions to ask of the text:

- What is the photographer trying to convey with this image?
- Can a photographer convey his or her own ideas in the same way that a painter or writer can?
- Can art represent truth?
- Can an artist capture extreme human emotions?
- To what extent are photographs 'composed'?
- Is photography literal, or can it have symbolic significance?
- Does photography such as Ponomarev's 'elevate the imagination', or is its purpose very different?

ACTIVITY

Think about what answers you might give to these questions.

Leah then read several online interviews with Sergey Ponomarev and noted the following phrases:

> 'Ponomarev is no romantic. He is a working conflict photographer.'
>
> 'I was with them [the refugees] and not with them at the same time.'
>
> 'Many of them [the refugees] did understand that they are a part of a key historical event, and that we were only trying to publicize their story – maybe even generate some help.'
>
> 'There were many hard moments.'
>
> 'Pressure and uncertainty'
>
> 'Nobody <u>really</u> knows what they're doing or where they're going.'
>
> 'I pitied them.'
>
> 'Photography used to have ... a serious impact on public opinion. Now we have the internet users who randomly scroll across endless pages and occasionally come across a photo from a war that shows dead bodies or drowned children or bombed houses. Instead of being distressed and enraged by the imagery, these users are more likely to get worked up because the scenes are ruining their morning coffee.'

ACTIVITY

In your learner profile, answer the following questions in note form:

- **What area of study would you focus on after reading these notes?**
- **How would you make sense of the material Leah has collected?**
- **What would you advise Leah to do next?**

Keep reading, keep researching, keep taking notes. Although it is sometimes tempting to think that you have done enough preparation, it is always worth following a lead, reading more widely and pushing yourself to think about the ideas you are exploring. This stage takes time, but it is always worthwhile!

Leah continued to read (among others) Geoff Dyer, John Berger, Roland Barthes and Susan Sontag. She added notes to her learner profile. Here is a sample of some of those notes, all taken from Susan Sontag's book *On Photography*:

> 'Photographs <u>cannot create a moral position</u>, but they can <u>reinforce</u> one – and can help build a nascent one.'
>
> '... there is <u>something predatory in the act of taking a picture</u>. To photograph people is to <u>violate</u> them, by seeing them as they never see themselves, by having knowledge of them that they can never have; it <u>turns people into objects</u> that can be <u>symbolically possessed</u>.'
>
> '<u>The painter constructs, the photographer discloses</u>.'
>
> 'Photographs are a way of imprisoning reality ... One <u>can't possess reality, one can possess images</u> – one can't possess the present but one can possess the past.'

ACTIVITY

In your learner portfolio, write down why you think Leah has underlined these phrases: Do you agree with Sontag's comments? How applicable are they to Ponomarev's work?

Wider reading can benefit your knowledge and understanding of a subject you are studying, but it can also open up new and fascinating lines of enquiry. You may not be familiar with some of the authors mentioned in this section, but this could be a good opportunity to note their names in your learner portfolio and explore them later.

KEY CONCEPT

Remember that your line of enquiry should explore *one* of the seven concepts from the English A: Language and Literature course: creativity, culture, community, identity, perspective, transformation and representation.

Stage 3: establishing your line of enquiry

A good line of enquiry directs you towards a meaningful engagement with a text. It should be an argument, not a description, and it should provide you with an opportunity to explore both the author's purpose and the reader's response.

Leah used various strategies to access these complex issues. She talked to others about what these images showed us today. She asked them questions inspired by her reading of Barnes and Sontag, and noted down their responses in her learner profile.

She narrowed down her possible lines of enquiry to four.

	Key concept: Community
Line of enquiry	1 To what extent does Sergey Ponomarev's work represent the reality of the Syrian refugee crisis?
	2 Through which pictorial devices does Ponomarev explore the theme of community in his photographs of the refugee crisis?
	3 In what ways and for what reasons does Ponomarev explore community in his work on the refugee crisis?
	4 To what extent is photography lacking the artistic freedom to convey universal truths about human experience that other art forms are able to achieve?
Hook	In conversations with others (family members, friends, teachers, fellow students), discuss what these images show us today.

	Key concept: Community
Relevance	Why are these pictures relevant to all of us today? What global issues do they explore? Discuss these in pairs or as a group, and write notes in your learner portfolio on ideas that you think could help you with your essay.
Thesis statement	This essay will explore how the artistic limitations of photography can demand that artists explore universal issues using different approaches to representation.

ACTIVITY

Which of Leah's four possible lines of enquiry do you think will lead her to write the most effective essay? Why?

REFLECT

The line of enquiry may be seen as an opportunity for you to explore an area of interest beyond the set texts you are studying. What are you passionate about? What might you want to study in the future? Such questions are worth asking, because researching a subject and writing about something at such length, is easier when you have a motivating interest or curiosity.

Stage 4: planning your HL essay

Leah continued to read around her subject. After this research, she felt that she was in a good position to start planning her essay.

AREAS OF EXPLORATION

Remember to use the areas of exploration as 'lenses' through which to approach different texts. How will you address, both implicitly and explicitly, a range of these questions in your HL essay?

As she planned her essay, Leah noted down some of the 18 guiding questions that she felt could bring her analysis into sharper focus:

Readers, writers and texts:

How are we affected by texts in various ways?
In what ways is meaning discovered, constructed and expressed?
How do texts offer both insights and challenges?

Time and space:
How important is cultural context to the production and perception of a text?
To what extent do texts offer insight into another culture?
How do texts engage with local and global issues?

Intertextuality: connecting texts

How can texts offer multiple perspectives of a single issue, topic or theme?

Make a list of other guiding questions you might consult as you plan the essay.

Leah decided to write an essay on the fourth line of enquiry: 'To what extent is photography lacking the artistic freedom to convey universal truths about human experience that other art forms are able to achieve?'

Before she started writing her essay, she wrote a synopsis of her argument:

Synopsis:
This essay will analyse the work of Sergey Ponomarev, and in particular the images he took of the refugee crisis in southern Europe. My argument will be that although visual texts such as Ponomarev's are less crafted than similar images – such as Géricault's 'The Raft of the Medusa' – they can still convey truths which are universal to the human condition. The 'interpretative relationship' – traditionally between author and reader – is shifted more towards the latter as meaning is constructed by those who encounter the text, rather than the author, or those captured in the moment. The 'reader' discovers, constructs and expresses meaning from the image, but this is dependent, to some extent, on the prior experience that the reader has had with the cultures being represented and the understanding of the global issues being explored. A painter like Géricault is more able to include symbolism than a photographer, but by referencing the critical work of Sontag I will argue that symbolism is implicit and explicit and created by the reader.

Based on this synopsis, write an introduction to an essay which responds to Leah's line of enquiry. Remember to contextualise your argument at the start of the essay, and include your line of enquiry. You should also include your thesis statement in the opening paragraph to make your argument clear.

Stage 5: writing your HL essay

After consulting with her teacher, Leah felt that she had done enough preparation to begin writing her essay. By following this five-stage approach, Leah felt confident that she was able to write an informed and balanced HL essay. However, she knew that, in order for the essay to be effective, she had to remain self-critical of her own writing.

For example, this is Leah's first attempt at the opening paragraph of her essay:

The refugee crisis of 2015 was one of the greatest humanitarian challenges the world has ever faced. Thousands fled Syria and North Africa, risking their lives in the process. And many died. News agencies, journalists, photographers and film makers attempted to represent the scale of the tragedy, but it could be argued that it was beyond comprehension for most people not involved in the events themselves. The challenge for those who do wish to effect change is finding the images, and words, to influence public opinion enough to change political will. In this sense artists can play a vital role in improving humanitarian crises. This raises the line of enquiry: to what extent is photography lacking the artistic freedom to convey universal truths about human experience that other art forms are able to achieve? This essay will explore how the artistic limitations of photography can demand artists to explore universal issues using different approaches to representation.

Peer-assessment

By referring back to the assessment criteria for the HL essay provided earlier in this section, how would you mark Leah's opening paragraph? Think about the strong points in her work, and where she may lose some marks.

After Leah had discussed this first draft of her opening paragraph with her teacher, the following action points were agreed:

- Make the opening clearer and more succinct.

- Avoid making generalised statements.

- Improve the points of transition from the general introduction to the line of enquiry and the thesis statement.

Here is Leah's second draft, in which she addresses these action points:

> The refugee crisis of 2015 was one of the greatest humanitarian challenges the modern age has ever confronted. It has been estimated by the United Nations that in that year alone nearly 4000 migrants died trying to cross the Mediterranean. In order to effect change political will had to be influenced, and artists – be they writers, film makers, photographers or actors – would have to contribute to this process. But are some forms of art better at changing public opinion than others? And is this outcome more suited to the activist and politician, rather than the artist? Photographers often report from the front line, but asking if this medium is more constrained than other methods of expression is an interesting line of enquiry to pursue because it also asks us to explore if there are certain forms of expression that are better able to represent subjective and objective truth. To put it another way: if photography is a one-dimensional representation of experience, is it so limited – compared to painting or literature – that it cannot convey real complexity? Sergey Ponomarev tried to capture the experiences of refugees in 2015, and this will form the basis of this analysis.

ACTIVITY

Why do you think the teacher felt this second attempt was a stronger opening than the first draft?

Can you improve it still further? If so, what three points would you suggest to Leah about strengthening her opening?

In your learner portfolio, write the second and third paragraphs of this essay.

Self-assessment

Once you have finished writing the second and third paragraphs of the essay, read them again and ask yourself:

- Have you addressed the assessment criteria for the HL essay (listed at the start of this section)?

- Have you made use of the approaches suggested so far in this section?

You might also swap your work with a fellow student, and give feedback on each other's paragraphs.

Writing your HL essay on literature

You may choose to write your HL essay on a literary text. In the second part of this section, we will take you through the process of choosing a text, planning a response, and carefully structuring an essay on poetry, using the same five-stage approach that we used when looking at writing a non-literary essay.

Stage 1: preliminary reading and research

Remember that you can write your HL essay on any of the texts you have studied in your course, as long as you haven't used them in any of the other assessments. If you decide to write your HL essay on a literary text then it could be from any genre. This section will focus particularly on writing about poetry, and you will be able to read the specific texts on which the sample material is based.

If you are writing your essay about poetry, then you will probably have studied at least 15 poems by the poet you have chosen. You will not, however, be able to refer to all of these in your essay. Therefore, you will need to be selective.

Stage 2: focused reading and research

The next stage in preparing your HL essay is to complete some careful research. In the following worked example, we will refer to five separate poems by William Blake, an English poet writing at the end of the 18th century. Blake was a poet, but also an artist and printmaker. His poems have been reproduced here in their original form, from his 'illuminated books'.

ACTIVITY

Read the following poems by Blake. Annotate them carefully and think about ways in which you might be able to make connections between them.

REFLECT

Although you wouldn't necessarily need to comment on Blake's illustrations as well as the language of his poems in an HL essay, it is interesting to consider how the two art forms work together. What do you think the original illustrated versions add to the poems?

The Garden of Love

I went to the Garden of Love,
And saw what I never had seen:
A Chapel was built in the midst,
Where I used to play on the green.

And the gates of this Chapel were shut,
And Thou shalt not. writ over the door;
So I turn'd to the Garden of Love,
That so many sweet flowers bore.

And I saw it was filled with graves,
And tomb-stones where flowers should be:
And Priests in black gowns, were walking their rounds,
And binding with briars, my joys & desires.

London

I wander thro' each charter'd street,
Near where the charter'd Thames does flow.
And mark in every face I meet
Marks of weakness, marks of woe.

In every cry of every Man,
In every Infant's cry of fear,
In every voice: in every ban,
The mind-forg'd manacles I hear

How the Chimney-sweepers cry
Every blackning Church appalls,
And the hapless Soldier's sigh
Runs in blood down Palace walls

But most thro' midnight streets I hear
How the youthful Harlots curse
Blasts the new-born Infant's tear
And blights with plagues the Marriage hearse.

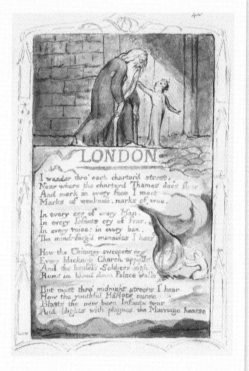

The Sick Rose

O Rose thou art sick.
The invisible worm,
That flies in the night
In the howling storm:

Has found out thy bed
Of crimson joy:
And his dark secret love
Does thy life destroy.

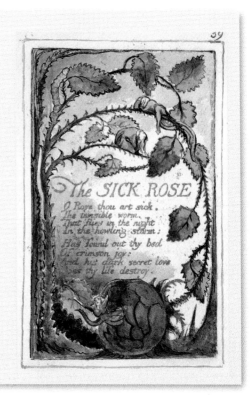

A Poison Tree

I was angry with my friend;
I told my wrath, my wrath did end.
I was angry with my foe:
I told it not, my wrath did grow.

And I waterd it in fears,
Night & morning with my tears:
And I sunned it with smiles,
And with soft deceitful wiles.

And it grew both day and night.
Till it bore an apple bright.
And my foe beheld it shine,
And he knew that it was mine.

And into my garden stole,
When the night had veild the pole;
In the morning glad I see:
My foe outstretched beneath the tree.

The Tyger

Tyger Tyger, burning bright,

In the forests of the night;

What immortal hand or eye,

Could frame thy fearful symmetry?

In what distant deeps or skies

Burnt the fire of thine eyes?

On what wings dare he aspire?

What the hand, dare seize the fire?

And what shoulder, & what art,

Could twist the sinews of thy heart?

And when thy heart began to beat,

What dread hand? & what dread feet?

What the hammer? what the chain,

In what furnace was thy brain?

What the anvil? what dread grasp,

Dare its deadly terrors clasp!

When the stars threw down their spears

And water'd heaven with their tears:

Did he smile his work to see?

Did he who made the Lamb make thee?

Tyger Tyger burning bright,

In the forests of the night:

What immortal hand or eye,

Dare frame thy fearful symmetry?

Stage 3: establishing your line of enquiry

As you start planning your literary HL essay, you will need to decide on a *line of enquiry*. It is important that you do this at the same time as choosing the material that you will refer to in the essay.

The title of a collection or book is often an excellent starting point for considering the line of enquiry that you are going to take. All of these poems come from Blake's collection *Songs of Innocence and Experience*. So, you could start planning a possible line of enquiry by thinking about the following:

- The words 'innocence' and 'experience' clearly map out a potential conflict or site of tension.

- The title seems to invite the reader to think about the world from different, and opposing, perspectives.

Higher-level essay

- There seems to be a clear ethical dimension registered in this contrast.
- 'Innocence' suggests more than naivety, and perhaps implies a morally positive view of the world.
- 'Experience', on the other hand, suggests more than just wisdom and longevity, and perhaps implies a morally compromised view of the world.

Taking this as a starting point, you can interrogate the tensions in the collection's title and use them to help shape your line of enquiry and, ultimately, your HL essay question.

REFLECT

As you think about the various works that you have studied throughout the course, which do you think are most likely to provide you with a clear line of enquiry? And which do you think you would most enjoy writing about in an HL essay?

You might, for example, use the tensions identified in the title of Blake's work to ask a question like this:

'*How does Blake present the tension between innocence and experience in his poems?*'

However, while this question would make for an interesting essay, it might be rather too broad. You should make your essay focus as specific as possible. Therefore, you might try to re-focus it, zooming in on the particular themes of the Blake poems you've chosen to write about. Thinking about those poems, perhaps one area of interest to explore might be that of personal freedom. Therefore, you can develop the idea of the focused question one step further and ask:

'*How does Blake present the limitations of personal freedom in the collection* Songs of Innocence and Experience*?*'

This question should help you focus on some very specific aspects of the poems.

Remember, you may find that you want to keep refining your title further, as you write the essay. By doing this, you can continue to make it even more focused and specific.

ACTIVITY

Have a go at writing your own essay question for one of the texts that you are considering using for your HL essay.

Choosing quotations

ACTIVITY

Read the Blake poems carefully and make notes on them.

When you are preparing for the HL essay, you should read your chosen text(s) again and carefully collate the evidence you will use in the essay to address your thesis statement and answer the question. This evidence will usually take the form of carefully chosen quotations.

As you read your texts again in preparation for writing the HL essay, you need to focus on selecting quotations which you can use as evidence to support your argument. You should aim to:

- pick quotations that are as short as possible, while still providing the evidence that you will need
- wherever possible, select quotations that are linguistically or formally interesting in order to support your analysis and evaluation of language and form
- make a note of the context of the quotations, and exactly where they come from, so that you can reference them later in the essay.

TIP

Determining your HL essay question

When planning for your HL essay, remember that a good question should:

- be phrased *as a question*
- be appropriate, specific and focused
- invite the writer to respond personally in terms of constructing a clear thesis or argument.

TIP

The easiest way to demonstrate that you know your chosen literary work is to provide evidence from the text, in the form of quotations, to support the points that you are making. Carefully selected quotations from your texts should provide the backbone to your HL essay.

Writing an introduction

The first thing that the person marking your HL essay will read will be your introduction. However, it will not necessarily be the first thing that you write. You will definitely need to have planned what you intend to say in each paragraph before you write the introduction. You will certainly want to return to it during the drafting process, to make sure that it is clearly addressing the terms of the question and setting out a very specific thesis which will provide the focus for your essay.

Sample response

Read this sample introduction, written by a student, and then answer the questions that follow.

> In 'Songs of Innocence and Experience' William Blake presents personal freedom and autonomy of action as being limited by the restricting interventions of authorities. In 'The Garden of Love' and 'London' Blake presents the controlling behaviours of institutions and authority figures as limiting individual rights and liberties. In 'The Sick Rose' and 'A Poison Tree', we are presented with the personal suffering that can result from societal action; in comparison, 'The Tyger' asks critical questions about who or what is responsible for our freedoms. All of these poems present personal freedoms as under threat or having been destroyed, and offer a bleak view of a world of 'experience' without the individual liberties enjoyed in 'innocence'.

REFLECT

- Given that the essay as a whole must be no longer than 1500 words, do you think this introduction is about the right length (about 100 words)?

- How far does the introduction address the question head-on and construct a clear thesis to help focus the essay? How clear is that thesis in the final sentence?

- Although an introduction need not list the specific poems or areas of the text that will be the focus of the essay, do you think it is helpful to do this here? Why?

ACTIVITY

Have a go at writing your own introduction of about 100 words on one of the texts that you are considering using for your HL essay. Use the question that you planned earlier and draw on the sample introduction above as a model.

TIP

Time spent planning your HL essay is always time well spent. You should aim not to start writing your essay until you have planned exactly what you intend to say in your thesis and in each of your paragraphs.

Stage 4: planning your HL essay

Before you start writing, you will need to have planned your essay very carefully, including what you will argue in each paragraph. Given that the essay has a maximum length of 1500 words, you should be writing no more than four or five 'body' paragraphs. In your plan, you should decide for each of these paragraphs:

- what your topic sentence will be, and how it will link back to your thesis and the essay question

- which quotations you will use and in what order

- how you will ensure that you include analysis and evaluation in your writing.

3

Read the following paragraph from the same student's HL essay. As you read, note the structure of the paragraph, how it uses quotations, and how it addresses the assessment criteria. The paragraph has been annotated to help you identify key aspects of its structure.

> The paragraph starts with a topic sentence which aims to refer back to the essay title, fit in with the essay's overall thesis, and operate as a micro-argument for the paragraph

> The paragraph then provides the reader with some context about the first poem being discussed and immediately quotes from the poem as evidence as well as offering analytical and evaluative comments about the language quoted

> As the paragraph develops, it offers a clear interpretation of the poem in response to the essay question and the focus suggested in the topic sentence. The constant referencing of the language of the poem demonstrates the student's knowledge and understanding and the commentary on the effect of the language quoted aims to be both analytical and evaluative

> The paragraph aims to identify literary features (here we can see metaphor being discussed) and to analyse and evaluate their various effects. With poetry it is also particularly important to talk about form, and here the paragraph analyses the effect of rhyme

Blake's poems demonstrate how individual freedoms are restricted by the actions of authorities whose controlling behaviours limit individual autonomy of action. In 'The Garden of Love', for example, the narrator re-visits a place of peace and tranquillity from his youth; it is an environment which, in the past, bore 'so many sweet flowers'. Flowers represents happiness, freedom and the flourishing of nature and the qualifying adjective 'sweet' marks them out also as symbols of innocence. However, this is a description of an earlier, innocent moment, and the present reality that is described is much bleaker and repressive. Indeed, in the garden, there is a church but we find out that 'the gates of this Chapel were shut'. Here the 'gates' operate as an obvious symbol of exclusion: the locked building denies access to the narrator in a physical act of restricting personal freedom. This is further reinforced by the biblical quotation 'writ over the door' stating: 'Thou shalt not'. The religious authorities have stamped a restrictive message over the portal of the chapel, reiterating the levels of control being inflicted which is further underlined by the patrolling figures of the 'Priests in black gowns' who are 'walking their rounds,/ And binding with briars, my joys & desires.' The final line of the final stanza of the poem employs the metaphor of the sinister 'briars' (prickly plants which could cause damage) stifling the narrator's personal freedom and the internal rhyme ('briars' and 'desires') ironically pulls together the aspiration for freedom and the thing that is restricting it. There is a similar image used in another poem of experience, 'London' where the narrator hears in 'every cry' in the street around him, 'mind-forg'd manacles'. Here the metaphor is more concrete - manacles are literally handcuffs, forging is the physical process of making something out of metal - and the image is made more insidious by the suggestion that the restrictions are 'mind-forged', almost as if the narrator has been the victim of authoritarian brain-washing. As the patrolling priests, marked out as restricting authorities by their sinister 'black gowns', exert control, here we can see individual freedoms and individual autonomy of action being cruelly restricted.

> The paragraph takes its examples from more than one poem in order to show knowledge and understanding of the collection as a whole but also to make connections between different poems

> As the paragraph comes to a conclusion, it re-focuses on the areas identified in the topic sentences and aims to ensure that it is very specifically answering the question

Addressing the assessment criteria in your HL essay

As you are planning your HL essay, you should aim to ensure that every paragraph addresses the assessment criteria as specifically as possible. At both the planning and the writing stages, you should check that each paragraph demonstrates effective use of:

- knowledge, understanding and interpretation
- analysis and evaluation
- focus, organisation and development
- language.

Stage 5: writing your HL essay

Once you have completed your planning, you will be ready to start writing the essay. In doing so, you will need to focus specifically on addressing the assessment criteria.

ACTIVITY

Now read the next paragraph of the student's sample HL essay on William Blake. Make your own annotations in response to the questions on the right of the exemplar paragraph, making sure that you are thinking carefully about how the writing specifically addresses the assessment criteria.

Sample response

Blake's poems present personal freedoms being corroded by the devastating effects of the actions of society on the individual. In 'The Sick Rose', for instance, Blake uses the powerful image of a rose to represent something that should be a symbol of strength and beauty but which has been destroyed. Its freedom to flourish has been compromised by an 'invisible worm,/ That flies in the night'. The symbolism is both persuasive and ambivalent: the 'worm' could be a representation of the devil as a serpent from the bible, but it could equally be an undercover ('invisible') agent of the state. Its clandestine qualities are foregrounded in the poem's descriptions of it acting in 'the night', an obvious metaphor for secrecy, subterfuge and deceit. In the case of 'the howling storm', the metaphor suggests a dangerous, revolutionary moment where the onomatopoeic 'howling' underlines the apparent physical pain and suffering being experienced. All of these actions have 'found out' the person being addressed in the poem and, in the final lines, we discover that this 'dark secret love' has destroyed his life, if not literally, then certainly in terms of no longer possessing the freedoms to act in line with his hopes and desires. A similar sense of corrosive internal inhibition is presented in 'A Poison Tree' where the narrator's 'wrath' or anger is represented as a metaphorical tree which grows as a symbol of that anger. This secretive, internal destruction is ironically presented when the anger (the tree) is being nurtured by the narrator as he 'sunned it with smiles,/ And with soft deceitful wiles'. It is ironic because these apparently positive and nurturing actions (the warming of the sun, smiling, softness) are causing the tree - the anger - to grow internally and dangerously. The tree ultimately causes the death of the poem's antagonist in a chillingly literal representation of the curtailing of freedoms.

Annotation questions:

How does the paragraph's topic sentence help with the 'focus, organisation and development' of the essay?

How does the paragraph's use of quotation demonstrate 'knowledge, understanding and interpretation'?

How is the paragraph demonstrating skills of 'analysis and evaluation'? If evaluation is the weighing up of different pieces of evidence and interpretations then how is this paragraph specifically being evaluative?

How does the paragraph use specific literary terminology in order to support its analysis?

How is the language of the paragraph appropriate to the form of a literary essay?

Does the paragraph succeed in ensuring that it is consistently focused and organised, and developing the argument of the essay as a whole?

Writing a conclusion

The final paragraph of your essay will be a conclusion. It should be a short paragraph which shows how you have answered the question and resolves your argument. It may be no more than two or three sentences long, but it should refer back to the question and to your original thesis as set out in the introduction.

Worked full sample HL essay

In the following worked example, the student has written an essay on the following five poems by the English poet and novelist Thomas Hardy, who was writing at the start of the 20th century.

The Convergence of the Twain

I

In a solitude of the sea

Deep from human vanity,

And the Pride of Life that planned her, stilly couches she.

II

Steel chambers, late the pyres

Of her salamandrine fires,

Cold currents thrid, and turn to rhythmic tidal lyres.

III

Over the mirrors meant

To glass the opulent

The sea-worm crawls — grotesque, slimed, dumb, indifferent.

IV

Jewels in joy designed

To ravish the sensuous mind

Lie lightless, all their sparkles bleared and black and blind.

V

Dim moon-eyed fishes near

Gaze at the gilded gear

And query: 'What does this vaingloriousness down here?' ...

VI

Well: while was fashioning

This creature of cleaving wing,

The Immanent Will that stirs and urges everything

VII

Prepared a sinister mate

For her – so gaily great –

A Shape of Ice, for the time far and dissociate.

VIII

And as the smart ship grew

In stature, grace, and hue,

In shadowy silent distance grew the Iceberg too.

IX

Alien they seemed to be;

No mortal eye could see

The intimate welding of their later history,

X

Or sign that they were bent

By paths coincident

On being anon twin halves of one august event,

XI

Till the Spinner of the Years

Said 'Now!' And each one hears,

And consummation comes, and jars two hemispheres.

The Darkling Thrush

I leant upon a coppice gate
　　When Frost was spectre-grey,
And Winter's dregs made desolate
　　The weakening eye of day.
The tangled bine-stems scored the sky
　　Like strings of broken lyres,
And all mankind that haunted nigh
　　Had sought their household fires.

The land's sharp features seemed to be
　　The Century's corpse outleant,
His crypt the cloudy canopy,
　　The wind his death-lament.
The ancient pulse of germ and birth
　　Was shrunken hard and dry,
And every spirit upon earth
　　Seemed fervourless as I.

At once a voice arose among
　　The bleak twigs overhead
In a full-hearted evensong
　　Of joy illimited;
An aged thrush, frail, gaunt, and small,
　　In blast-beruffled plume,
Had chosen thus to fling his soul
　　Upon the growing gloom.

So little cause for carolings
　　Of such ecstatic sound
Was written on terrestrial things
　　Afar or nigh around,
That I could think there trembled through
　　His happy good-night air
Some blessed Hope, whereof he knew
　　And I was unaware.

31 December 1900

The Voice

Woman much missed, how you call to me, call to me,
Saying that now you are not as you were
When you had changed from the one who was all to me,
But as at first, when our day was fair.

Can it be you that I hear? Let me view you, then,
Standing as when I drew near to the town
Where you would wait for me: yes, as I knew you then,
Even to the original air-blue gown!

Or is it only the breeze, in its listlessness
Travelling across the wet mead to me here,
You being ever dissolved to wan wistlessness,
Heard no more again far or near?

　　Thus I; faltering forward,
　　Leaves around me falling,
Wind oozing thin through the thorn from norward,
　　And the woman calling.

In Time of 'The Breaking of Nations'

I

Only a man harrowing clods
    In a slow silent walk
With an old horse that stumbles and nods
    Half asleep as they stalk.

II

Only thin smoke without flame
    From the heaps of couch-grass;
Yet this will go onward the same
    Though Dynasties pass.

III

Yonder a maid and her wight
    Come whispering by:
War's annals will cloud into night
    Ere their story die.

1900

The Man He Killed

"Had he and I but met
    By some old ancient inn,
We should have sat us down to wet
    Right many a nipperkin!

"But ranged as infantry,
    And staring face to face,
I shot at him as he at me,
    And killed him in his place.

"I shot him dead because –
    Because he was my foe,
Just so: my foe of course he was;
    That's clear enough; although

"He thought he'd 'list, perhaps,
    Off-hand like – just as I –
Was out of work – had sold his traps –
    No other reason why.

"Yes; quaint and curious war is!
    You shoot a fellow down
You'd treat if met where any bar is,
    Or help to half-a-crown."

1902

The HL essay that you are about to read is written in response to the question:
'How do Thomas Hardy's poems present the relationship between the personal and the public?'

Read the essay and the accompanying comments carefully.

In Hardy's poetry the personal and the public, the ordinary and the extraordinary, are juxtaposed. In this way, Hardy presents the reader with a stoic picture of life continuing as normal even in the shadow of catastrophic events in the history of humanity. The poems celebrate that ordinariness while also mourning the tragedy of war and of loss. In doing so they register, on the one hand, the resilience of humanity and of nature in continuing despite tragedy, loss, and great suffering, but also the vanity of some human behaviour and its tragic consequences.

In 'The Convergence of the Twain' (subtitled 'Lines on the loss of the Titanic') Hardy presents the jarring of 'two hemispheres' as the Titanic and the iceberg converge and lead to the destruction of the famous liner. The poem explores the convergence of the mechanical and man-made with nature and presents the natural world as continuing as usual even in the face of a terrible human tragedy. The Titanic is presented by Hardy as a metaphor for the unstoppable progress of industrialisation, full of 'pyres/ Of her salamandrine fires'. But the power of the rhetorical presentation of this majestical strength is ironically undercut as the ship is, in fact, stilled in 'a solitude of the sea' at the bottom of the ocean and is also an act of 'Human vanity'. The poem employs a series of images to show the futility of the trappings of luxury in the wake of the disaster. For example, jewels 'designed/ To ravish the sensuous mind/ Lie lightless', where the alliteration glitters ironically to underscore the darkness of the bottom of the ocean. In the hull of the sunk ship there are 'mirrors meant/ To glass the opulent' but these are now the playground of the 'sea-worm'. In contrast to opulence, we are presented with something 'grotesque, slimed' but also 'dumb' (there is no noise) and 'indifferent': nature has reduced the grandiloquence of the Titanic to something indistinguishable from nature. Or, in the view of the 'Dim moon-eyed fishes' that Hardy imagines, they are musing philosophically (while gazing at the elaborate alliterative 'gilded gear') 'What does this vaingloriousness down here?' drawing attention to the vanity of human behaviour and its tragic results. This sense of the world continuing as usual in despite of great human tragedies is equally captured in 'In Time of the Breaking of Nations' where the narrator tells us how: 'this will go onward the same/ Though Dynasties pass.' In 'The Convergence of the Twain' this is because 'No mortal eye could see/ The intimate welding of their later history'. Human or 'mortal' life is subservient to the great power of the natural world.

'In Time of the Breaking of Nations' celebrates the preservation and refusal to be put down of the ordinary and quotidian in the face of the terrible consequences of war. In the poem, the war is a distant murmur that barely registers its presence in an unchanging natural world. The first stanza starts with the image of a 'man harrowing clods/ In a slow silent walk'. The alliterative adjectives 'slow' and 'silent' conveys the solitude and the peace of the situation. Here we are presented with a very ordinary farmer engaged in the act of 'harrowing clods' (turning over the soil) accompanied by a plainly and simply described 'old horse'. That horse also represents the eerily quiet atmosphere as he 'stumbles and nods/ Half asleep'. There's an automatic, detached quality to the actions of both farmer and

---

In the introduction, the essay sets out a thesis in response to the question. The final sentence operates as a 'thesis statement' which sets out a focused argument for the essay as a whole

This topic sentence immediately signals the poem that will be the focus for the paragraph

In analysing the poem, the student here addresses Criterion A in making use of short, embedded quotations to evidence the points being made

As this paragraph zooms in to explore the effects of the poem's language, it uses technical terms and references literary devices in order to support the analysis

The paragraph retains its focus on answering the question and addresses Criterion C in connecting and developing ideas in referencing quotations from elsewhere in the collection of poems, as supporting evidence for the points being made.

The next body paragraph tackles a different poem, but one that has already been mentioned in the essay

Here the essay zooms in to examine language closely again and addresses Criterion B as it analyses and evaluates its effectiveness

horse and 'stumbles' suggests a lack of precise focus which is underlined by the dream-like state of 'Half asleep'. Life carries on as normal, Hardy tells us: 'this will go onward the same/ Though Dynasties pass.' This switch from the micro to the macro, from the small details of the farmer's life to the sweep of history suggested by dynasties passing, reminds the reader that this is a poem written during the First World War; indeed, as the poem's title poignantly has it: 'In Time of the Breaking of Nations'. The destructive power of 'Breaking' is contrasted in the final stanza by the barely noticed 'whispering' of 'a maid and her wight': a young couple, in love, oblivious to the world around them. In fact, that couple are presented as a model of the intransigence of love and normality: the poem's tone is overwhelmingly sad and yet its final couplet tells us that: 'War's annals will cloud into night/ Ere their story die.' The persistence of humanity, of love, and of the resolutely ordinary ('their story' is that of the emblematic lovers) will outlast the 'annals' of war and the present terrible moment of 'Breaking of Nations' will ultimately be subsumed into history.

The structure and focus of this paragraph and its connections to the argument and development of the thesis set out in the introduction address Criterion C

This presentation of war is similarly presented in 'The Man he Killed'. The poem tells the story of a soldier who has, in war, killed another man and it is a meditation on the tragic misfortune of that act. The final stanza starts with a wistful: 'Yes; quaint and curious war is!' The caesura after the first word – marked with the semi-colon – registers a sharp intake of breath, a taking stock before the ironic painting of war as 'quaint and curious'. These superficially slight adjectives speak to the terrible vicissitudes of circumstance: the speaker has killed someone who, in any other time 'Had he and I but met/ By some old ancient inn,/ We should have sat us down to wet/ Right many a nipperkin!' The conditional tense – 'We should have' – registers the tragic sense of what might have been in contrast to the brutal reality of the necessities of acting as required in war. This speaker, in monosyllabic, unadorned language, tells us: 'I shot at him as he at me/ And killed him in his place.' The precisely poignant 'in his place' captures the savage truths of war: that the rules of the ordinary are suspended and actions are reduced to apparently simply ethical decisions ('I shot him dead because —/ Because he was my foe'. Nevertheless, as one line bleeds into the next, the halting enjambment, the pause of the dash, and the awkward repetition of 'because', all suggest that this behaviour is not really, as the stanza ironically concludes, 'clear enough'. 'Because' suggests a simple relationship between cause and effect and yet the fact that the word sticks in the speaker's throat presents the deeply complex and disturbing morality of war. War is presented here through the prism and perspective of an ordinary man forced by the circumstances of conflict to act in an extraordinary way (to kill another man) when, in any normal situation rather than 'shoot a fellow down', you would help him 'to half-a-crown'. That final rhyme links the act of killing with a low value coin, foregrounding, as the poem ends, the tragic way in which war fails to value life and suspends and destroys the ordinary.

The essay continues to address Criterion A by making clear reference to the work being examined, by selecting helpful supporting examples and quotations

The essay continues to address Criterion D by using language that is effective for a literary essay and appropriately technical

Knowledge and understanding of the work are demonstrated by focusing on the specific qualities of the genre (poetry) chosen for the task, effectively addressing Criterion A

Hardy's presentation of the resilience of human existence is equally captured in 'The Darkling Thrush'. Here, the speaker observes a thrush singing on a barren winter's day. The landscape is presented bleakly: the 'Frost was spectre-grey', suggesting (with 'spectre') that there's an almost haunting desolation to the scene. Hope is embedded within the poem but it is hidden and unobtainable in the bleak present where: 'tangled bine-stems scored the sky/ Like strings of broken lyres'. Music, which we later see in the thrush's song, is trying to break out: the sky is

In referencing a number of different poems, the essay addresses Criterion A in demonstrating good knowledge and understanding of the work chosen

'scored' like a page of musical notation but as the simile extends the musical note, it compares nature to the broken strings of an instrument. The absence of the music is more powerfully felt by drawing attention to its possibility. Indeed, landscape is used to map out an historical moment when, in perhaps another reference to war, 'The land's sharp features' are presented as seeming 'to be/ The Century's corpse'. This metaphorical presentation of death means that there is 'little cause for carolings' or for 'ecstatic sound[s]'. And yet the thrush persists: 'His happy good-night air/ Some blessed Hope, whereof he knew/ And I was unaware.' The speaker seems to be compelled, even in the midst of doubt and depression, to acknowledge the possibility of hope (of which he is 'unaware') or, at least, the necessity of life going on. A similar effect is achieved in 'The Voice'. Its final stanza begins: 'Thus I; faltering forward,/ Leaves around me falling'. Once again we have a narrator who feels compelled by the forces of history. The opening 'Thus I' seems to register the inevitability of life and action and the alliterative 'faltering forward' suggests an inescapable march onward: the next step – the inevitable 'f' – will happen despite the 'faltering' nature of the progress among the falling leaves.

Hardy's poems present humanity at its best and worst. He paints a picture of rugged resilience but also of wanton 'vaingloriousness'. Life goes on in these poems, even despite terrible suffering and tragedy but the real hero is the natural world which continues with a resolute indifference to the vanity of human behaviour.

By continuing to employ technical and literary language, this paragraph continues to address Criterion D

By making links between different poems, the essay addresses Criterion C by connecting and developing ideas

The conclusion helps the essay to address Criterion C as it supports the structure of a formal literary essay as well as ensuring that the focus of the essay initially set out in the introduction has been maintained

Self- and peer-assessment

Return to the assessment criteria at the start of this section and assess this student's essay. Consider the following:

- How effective do you think this essay is in addressing each of the assessment criteria?
- If you were a teacher giving feedback to this student on their essay, in what ways would you suggest that the essay could be improved?

ACTIVITY

Having read the student's essay, and thought about how it might be assessed, try writing two paragraphs of your own on these Hardy poems.

Planning and writing your own HL essay

In this section, you have worked through all the stages of planning and writing an HL essay. You have read and assessed responses written by other students. You should now be in a good position to start planning and writing your own essay.

When planning and writing your essay, you should follow the advice of your teacher and your own class's deadlines. However, you might find it helpful to write an HL essay in your own time, for practice. You will need to consider the follow questions:

- Will your essay have a language or a literature focus?

- Which work or works will you write about?

- What will your line of enquiry be?

Once you've made these key decisions, then it's over to you to write either a practice essay or your final HL essay. Remember that, once you've finished writing, you should aim to spend some time, either on your own or with another student, assessing your work against the criteria and asking yourself how you can improve it even further.

Individual oral

In this section you will:

- remind yourself of the requirements of the IO and how it is assessed
- practise the skills needed to succeed in the IO
- examine examples of IOs and develop your critical awareness about what the oral exam requires of you.

4

- Develop your skills at choosing a global issue by taking an individual field of enquiry as your starting point.
- Improve your speaking skills by practising key elements of the IO.
- Understand the assessment criteria for the IO, and how to work with them effectively.
- Develop your own IO and outline.

Getting started

Your IO will focus on a global issue. When determining the global issue that you are going to address, you should make sure that it is:

- genuinely significant for many people
- important to people of many different nationalities
- something that affects our daily lives in a local context.

In order to start focusing on your global issue, you should begin by thinking about the following fields of enquiry:

- culture, identity and community
- beliefs, values and education
- politics, power and justice
- art, creativity and the imagination
- science, technology and the environment.

Think about how the texts you've studied during the course might fit into these broad fields of enquiry. Complete a copy of the grid below. You might be surprised about how many texts fit into more than one category!

Culture, identity and community	Beliefs, values and education	Politics, power and justice	Art, creativity and the imagination	Science, technology and the environment

Outline of assessment and task

Before we look at examples of IOs, let's remind ourselves of exactly what the task is and how it is assessed. As an English A: Language and Literature student (at both HL and SL) you will:

- choose a literary and a non-literary passage which are connected by a global issue of your choice
- choose extracts of up to 40 lines each from each text and bring an *unannotated* copy of both to your oral exam

- prepare an outline made up of ten bullet points in the form of notes to help you deliver your oral

- complete a 10-minute oral where you will speak for 5 minutes about each of the two prepared passages

- conclude the oral with a 5-minute discussion with your teacher.

There are four assessment criteria for the IO, which are the same for both SL and HL:

Criterion A	Knowledge, understanding and interpretation	10 marks
Criterion B	Analysis and evaluation	10 marks
Criterion C	Focus and organisation	10 marks
Criterion D	Language	10 marks
Total		40 marks

Choosing your texts and global issue

The first thing you need to do when starting to prepare your IO is to choose your texts and the global issue. In 'Sample individual oral 1', you'll see that although one text is a poem and the other non-fiction, they both take as their subject mankind's relationship with technology and the natural world. If you had chosen these two texts, there are a number of different fields of enquiry to help you get started. Let's imagine that you start, in this example, with 'Science, technology and the natural world'. The following steps demonstrate how you might start with a field of enquiry and arrive at a global issue:

1   The field of enquiry starting point is: Science and technology.

2   The specific focus from this field is: 'individual freedom and technology'.

3   In this example, you are thinking specifically about *how technology affects freedom*.

4   A further focus is on the *implications* for society.

5   Therefore, the final global issue is: the relationship between humans and the world they create, and how technology and the forces that shape it affect individual behaviour.

REFLECT

Think about your own use of social media:

- To what extent do you share your experiences with friends and family?

- Do you share ideas and opinions more widely using different platforms?

- How happy are you to share this information with the technology companies that build these programs?

- How accurately does your online profile reflect your personality?

Sample individual oral 1

Text 1: literature

Zeynep is studying history, English language and literature, and economics at higher level. She is also doing a world studies extended essay looking at how technology is impacting on democracy and the environment. During her studies, she read the poetry of the radical American poet Adrienne Rich. After studying Rich's poem 'What Kind of Times Are These' in class, Zeynep decided that, in order to have a coherent understanding of the text, she would first annotate the poem and then write a short commentary on it.

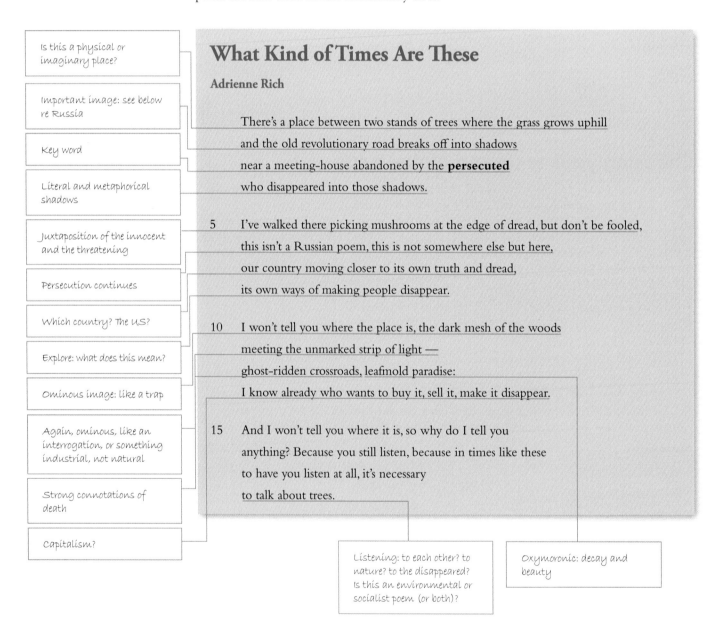

Annotations	Poem
Is this a physical or imaginary place?	**What Kind of Times Are These**
Important image: see below re Russia	Adrienne Rich
Key word	There's a place between two stands of trees where the grass grows uphill
Literal and metaphorical shadows	and the old revolutionary road breaks off into shadows
Juxtaposition of the innocent and the threatening	near a meeting-house abandoned by the **persecuted**
Persecution continues	who disappeared into those shadows.
Which country? The US?	5 I've walked there picking mushrooms at the edge of dread, but don't be fooled,
Explore: what does this mean?	this isn't a Russian poem, this is not somewhere else but here,
Ominous image: like a trap	our country moving closer to its own truth and dread,
Again, ominous, like an interrogation, or something industrial, not natural	its own ways of making people disappear.
Strong connotations of death	10 I won't tell you where the place is, the dark mesh of the woods
Capitalism?	meeting the unmarked strip of light —

ghost-ridden crossroads, leafmold paradise:

I know already who wants to buy it, sell it, make it disappear.

15 And I won't tell you where it is, so why do I tell you

anything? Because you still listen, because in times like these

to have you listen at all, it's necessary

to talk about trees.

Listening: to each other? to nature? to the disappeared? Is this an environmental or socialist poem (or both)?

Oxymoronic: decay and beauty

Here is the start of Zeynep's analysis of the poem.

> Adrienne Rich's poem is a powerful but ambiguous exploration of the dark forces that shape our world. Although the setting is rural (a wood) there are images, such as 'mesh' and 'strip of light', that are suggestive of something industrial. The location is 'a place between two stands of trees where the grass grows uphill', which is symbolic of a place between places, and also somewhere of struggle, an 'old revolutionary road' near an abandoned 'meeting-house'. The first verse, ominously, describes this as the location for some form of brutal action, where the 'persecuted' disappeared into 'shadows'.
>
> But Rich tells us that this is not Russia: this is 'our country' which is 'moving closer to its own truth and dread', with 'its own ways of making people disappear'. Rich keeps the exact location secret, but it is a place of death, a 'ghost-ridden ... leafmold paradise' which will be bought and sold. Perhaps the place is a piece of land which is sold by capitalists, wrecking its beauty, or politicians who have no understanding of its past. What Rich wants us to do, in these times when we are becoming increasingly disconnected, is to listen to each other, but also listen to nature, and to the trees. This is a poem about past secrets, but also of an ominous, dark present which, if we do not understand each other, threatens us all.

Here are Zeynep's teacher's comments on her opening analysis:

> Although short, this is an intelligent and perceptively written analysis of a complex and ambiguous poem. It is articulate, and explores many of the key images, drawing out from them the poem's key themes. More focus on literary technique, including structure, would have been helpful. This is very good preparation for the forthcoming individual oral.

TIP

Writing short commentaries on the texts you are considering using for the IO can help you get your ideas in order, and is also good practice for Paper 1.

Peer-assessment

- What do you think of Zeynep's analysis? What are its strengths and weaknesses?
- How useful do you find her teacher's comments?
- Is there anything you would add to Zeynep's commentary?
- What questions would you ask her teacher if you wanted to improve on Zeynep's work?

Text 2: language

Zeynep had been looking at non-fiction texts in class and was reading *The People Vs Tech: How the internet is killing democracy (and how we save it)* by Jamie Bartlett as part of her research for the extended essay. She decided that this extract would work well with Rich's poem. As with the literature text, Zeynep annotated this non-fiction text first, and then wrote a commentary on it.

As you read the following extract, ask yourself if Zeynep's annotations are making Bartlett's arguments clearer or not.

4

Annotations		Text
Any evidence for this assumption?		Without privacy laws – which vary greatly in force from country to country – we would today live in a world of total surveillance at all times.
Emotive, but again, what evidence is there?	5	In countries where such laws don't exist I fear it's almost certain that wearable tech, 'smart homes' and AI will create unprecedented levels of government surveillance and control. This is not only a worry in oligarchies or autocracies. In free societies we're never 'let alone' either; the data gold
Emotive phrase		rush has opened up new forms of potential surveillance from democratic governments, too, and most civil liberty groups worry what that means
What could happen (not what is happening?)		for legitimate political debate and activism. I, like many others, read with
But not all?	10	increasing alarm stories of people being arrested and prosecuted for saying things that are offensive and nasty, but no worse. In some cases
Like who? Name them...		intelligence agencies don't need to spy on you anymore; they can simply go to the technology companies and prise out of them what they need.
Are there any examples	15	There is another more subtle threat from Little Brother's constant surveillance and data sharing. Back in the eighteenth century, the
Emotive allusion, comic effect		philosopher Jeremy Bentham . . . proposed a new type of prison, which he called a 'panopticon'. It was designed so that all the inmates could
It was never created so we don't know if it would work	20	potentially be observed by a single watchman – without any knowledge of when they were being watched. The possibility alone was enough, thought Bentham, to ensure that everyone behaved. Our modern panopticon doesn't have just one watchman; everyone is both watching
So not a panopticon then?		and being watched. This kind of permanent visibility and monitoring is a way to enforce conformity and docility. Being always under surveillance
Is there evidence of this?	25	and knowing that the things you say are collected and shared creates a soft but constant self-censorship. It might not feel like that when people
What does 'soft' censorship mean? And don't all societies have some censorship?		are screaming abuse on Twitter – but for every angry troll there are hundreds of quiet users, lurkers who watch but don't post, for fear of the angry Twitter mob, the data collectors, a nosy employer or the hordes of professional offence-takers who shark around the net waiting to
How do we know? Perhaps these accounts are simply not used.	30	be upset.
What is? Not tweeting? The majority of people don't have Twitter accounts.	35	This is damaging to the citizen's ability to exercise moral judgement in their lives. Developing the faculties to think for oneself requires that people say controversial things, make mistakes and learn from them. But social media creates a strange form of performative politics, where we all act out certain roles and acceptable public responses (this idea is bad! This person is good!), which limits the room for genuine personal
Haven't we always done this? Haven't there always been witch hunts and 'us and them' mentalities?		growth. For example the ability to forget is an important part of self-development, because changing one's mind is how we are able to mature and grow. As an increasing number of people – both famous

| 40 | and not – have found to their cost, digital technology never forgets. Sometimes that has the benefit of uncovering powerful people's <u>motives and prejudices. But when one idiotic remark made on a</u> forum when you were young and ill-informed exists forever, and can be dug up and republished exactly as it was, more and more people | *So there are benefits* |
| 45 | will conclude it is safer just to never say anything. This is not a good environment of healthy, thinking adults. | *It could be because it is exactly what happened before Twitter. Unknowingly the author is effectively saying that democracy can't flourish without the ability to tweet which is a shallow interpretation of democracy* |

From The People Vs Tech: How the internet is killing democracy (and how we save it) by Jamie Bartlett

After writing her short commentaries, Zeynep decided to do a practice IO on these two texts. This was her ten-point plan:

1   State what the thesis statement is: connecting/becoming disconnected.

2   Explain why these two texts have been chosen.

3   Analyse Rich's poem, focusing on perspective and nature.

4   Discuss 'persecuted', 'disappeared', 'shadows': what do these mean?

5   Why isn't this a Russian poem? Repetition of 'disappear'.

6   Move to Bartlett text and the dangers of being monitored.

7   Explore the links between dictatorship and disappearing people.

8   Bartlett explains what a threat technology can be to democracy.

9   Environment is interpreted widely here: natural world, and also psychological.

10 Conclude.

TIP

Getting feedback on your text choices from your teacher is important, but other classmates can also provide you with valuable comments and suggestions. As you are allowed to bring brief notes with you into the IO, it is a good idea to discuss this with others in your class.

REFLECT

What do you think of this plan?

What would you retain, and what would you cut out, if you were planning an IO on these texts?

Zeynep decided to follow this structure, which had been worked on in class before. On the following pages is a condensed transcript of her practice IO, followed by the discussion with the teacher. The comments are added to give you additional guidance as you assess her response. The marks awarded are then given at the end.

The field of enquiry	Science, technology and the natural world
Global issue	The relationship between human beings and the natural world
Thesis statement	By being constantly connected, we risk becoming disconnected from our natural world.
Guiding question	How do texts engage with local and global issues?
What stylistic features or devices from the first text are relevant to the global issue?	Focus on specific technical aspects of Text 1
What stylistic features or devices from the second text are relevant to the global issue?	Focus on specific technical aspects of Text 2
Prompt	Examine the ways in which the global issue of your choice is presented through the content and form of two of the texts you have studied.

Good, clear articulation of the global issue

My global issue is science, technology and the natural world. I am particularly interested in the impact that technology has on the environment, and on our individual freedoms. I will argue that in being constantly connected we risk becoming disconnected from our natural world. The two texts that I have chosen – one by Adrienne Rich and the other by Jamie Bartlett – both explore these complex areas from different angles, but both, I feel, force us to think again about how we interact with the world around us, and each other.

Are these obviously linked?

Again, this seems a weak connection: are these texts well chosen?

Adrienne Rich's poem is a complex political poem. The setting is never specified, although she tells us that it is in the woods. She refers to a place between trees, an 'old revolutionary road' near an 'abandoned meeting house'. I think this suggests that nobody is meeting any more, because they are 'persecuted' or have disappeared into the shadows.

Good, but lacking in depth

Reasonable context, but the focus should be on the language

If you are familiar with modern history you might think about Stalin, or the disappeared of Chile, and other dictatorships which have seen opponents locked up or killed because they protested against the government. Rich was an American writer, but she does say that this threatening atmosphere could happen in 'our country', which could be anywhere.

Again, valid point, but is there enough evidence to support and extended analysis?

I think this is a poem not just about the threat to individual freedom, but also about nature. It's set in the woods, but there is something industrial about them: she uses imagery like 'mesh' and 'strip of light', which to me sounds like an interrogation room, not something beautiful. In the final verse she talks about how she knows who is going to buy it, and sell it, and

Possibly, but not a very strong image

make it disappear. The poem ends by asking us all to listen, not just to each other, but to the trees, which is our natural environment. This is a poem about politics, but also about the world around us.

The second text is linked to the Rich poem in a number of ways. Most obviously it is concerned with how we are all interconnected. But in this case the author, Jamie Bartlett, is looking much more clearly at technology. Bartlett makes several claims that are not always backed up by evidence, but for anyone actively involved in these issues they seem very obvious. He writes about how our individual freedoms are under threat from tech giants that monitor our movements through our mobile devices, or the websites we use. He also argues that social media, and in particular Twitter, is both guilty of creating a hysterical atmosphere and also of silencing voices, thus endangering free speech, because people are afraid of being attacked online.

One aspect that links both texts is that they both explore the environment, but in different ways. Rich writes about physical and geographical landscapes, and Bartlett describes the virtual environment, concluding that we now live 'not in a good environment' for 'healthy, thinking adults'. Bartlett's text is well structured and makes a number of very perceptive points. Like Rich, he places his arguments in historical context, referring specifically to Jeremy Bentham's panopticon.

I think this helps add extra power to his argument. It adds some perspective, and shows that the issues he is writing about are not new, but they are different from how they appeared before. There is literary context too, with an allusion to Orwell's 'Nineteen Eighty-Four'. Again, including such points adds greater depth to Bartlett's arguments, and makes it more persuasive.

Bartlett explores how, in our desire to remain constantly connected, we are at risk of throwing away our freedoms. We will become too scared to speak out for fear of having our information shared with those we don't want to see it. In many ways the themes are the same as Rich's poem: the disappeared in her poem are the silenced in Bartlett's text. But whereas in her poem these are dark acts done by others, in the extract from 'The People vs Tech' the absences are self-imposed. Both writers have a common solution: that we have to be brave, talk to others, reconnect with ourselves and with each other, and try to live in a healthy environment, whether that is online or in the real and physical world.

Again, this seems rather a weak connection between texts and doesn't really focus on the global issue

Mostly narrative, little analysis

Can these really be coupled together as the same environment?

Should be more specific

Not really exploring the arguments but seems to uncritically accept them

Again this seems rather weak: the comparisons are not clearly established

> **Teacher:** *Thank you. That was very interesting. I wonder if you could expand upon the point you make about the Bartlett extract being persuasive: would it not have been more so if the claims he made were evidenced?*
>
> **Zeynep:** *I think if you are familiar with the issues that he is writing about then such evidence is unnecessary. For example, he refers to the intelligence agencies being able to get information they need from tech companies by either forcing them to do so, or paying for it. Either way, they get what they want. I don't think you need footnotes giving examples of that because we all know it's true.*
>
> **Teacher:** *It may well be, but it is a complex area and I would have liked further information about how widespread this was. On first reading both texts appear rather bleak. Could I ask you about which text do you think is the most hopeful?*
>
> **Zeynep:** *I think the poem by Rich is. Although it seems, on the face of it, pretty dark, it does end with a positive tone. She asks us to listen, to ourselves, to trees, and I find that hopeful. I also think it's important to remember that those crimes are referred to mostly in the past by Rich, and even though she claims that 'our country' is moving closer to its own fate it isn't there yet, and there is still the chance of discussion and listening.*
>
> **Teacher:** *And you think that the Bartlett is less hopeful?*
>
> **Zeynep:** *Yes, because look at the forces he says are at work–and they are at work! The tech giants, the intelligence services, the fact that everyone has a mobile phone that is being tracked, all these things add up to a loss of privacy, and also puts freedom of speech at risk.*
>
> **Teacher:** *Which is the most effectively written text in your opinion?*
>
> **Zeynep:** *Well, of course they're doing different things: one is a poem, one if non-fiction. But if it is possible to evaluate both I would say that the most effective is the Bartlett. The reason I choose this is because both poems are written by activists, but really only one makes you want to take direct action, and that's the Bartlett. Of course, I don't know Rich's reasons for writing that poem, and it has qualities that the other one doesn't have–the atmosphere, for instance, is beautifully created–but I still think the Bartlett extract has a stronger impact on me.*

Two teachers listened to Zeynep's IO and agreed on the following feedback:

> The main problem with this oral was the choice of texts. Zeynep is interested in the issues involved, and is exploring them in her extended essay. She is an intelligent student who can analyse a text very effectively. Also, the annotations to both texts revealed a serious engagement with key points, but she chose to ignore her own ideas, and the advice of her teacher, in order to talk about two texts she liked. There were other concerns: the bullet points brought into the practice oral exam were underdeveloped, and the oral itself was too brief.

Sometimes texts don't work together, and preparing for the oral can take time and discussion. Very often, students have to choose different texts in order to bring the global issue into sharper focus. Some texts lend themselves to closer scrutiny because they overlap, not just in themes, but also in technique (even when one is literary and the other is not). Knowing the criteria, choosing the right texts and planning carefully how to structure the IO can all take time. But they can be very rewarding, not just in terms of the marks awarded, but intellectually as well.

Here is Zeynep's teacher's assessment of her performance.

Criterion A	Knowledge, understanding and interpretation	There is **some** knowledge of the extracts and the works in relation to the global issue, but too often the links seem tenuous and unsustained. The interpretation of both texts lacks real depth, and for Text 2 there is a reluctance to really challenge the arguments made. There are too few references to specific parts of both texts.
Criterion B	Analysis and evaluation	The oral contains **some** relevant analysis but is too reliant on description. The texts are identified, but are vaguely treated and only partially understood in relation to the presentation of the global issue – and to each other.
Criterion C	Focus and organisation	The oral does maintain a focus on the task, and on the works, but it is unbalanced, and the analysis is not consistently focused on shared ideas. There are **some** connections between ideas, but these are not always coherent.
Criterion D	Language	The language is clear and accurate; vocabulary and syntax are appropriate and varied; tone is appropriate to the task; technical terms are not used as often as they should have been.

Peer-assessment

After reading Zeynep's practice IO, and discussing it with a partner, how would you grade her performance? Base your marks on the assessment criteria.

The final marks awarded to Zeynep by her teacher were:

Criterion A: 4

Criterion B: 4

Criterion C: 4

Criterion D: 7

        19/40

ACTIVITY

Write a new ten-point plan for Zeynep's IO that is clearly focused on improving her response.

Sample individual oral 2

Text 1: literature

Lars is studying HL geography, English language and literature, and physics. During his studies, he became interested in the Extinction Rebellion movement that demands radical change to global environmental policies. He is also studying, as part of his course, the poetry of the English Romantic poets. For his literature text, he chose an extract from William Wordsworth's 'The Prelude'. He chose Greta Thunberg's climate speech for his language text, which we will look at later.

Global issue	Human relationships to nature and how they change over time
Thesis statement	Although both authors have very different perspectives, and come from very different times, there is a commonality of understanding of nature.
Guiding question	How have human relationships to nature changed from the time when Wordsworth was writing to the time of Greta Thunberg's speech, and how is that reflected in the texts?
What stylistic features or devices from the first text are relevant to the global issue?	Focus on key themes in Text 1
What stylistic features or devices from the second text are relevant to the global issue?	Focus on key themes in Text 2
Prompt	Examine the ways in which the global issue of your choice is presented through the content and form of two of the texts you have studied.

ACTIVITY

Before studying Lars's IO, annotate a copy of Wordsworth's poem yourself and see how much meaning you are able to draw from it.

REFLECT

Think about the activity, and your annotations to Wordsworth's poem.

- What did you struggle with?
- What did you enjoy exploring?
- Would this persuade you to use an older text or not?
- Does poetry – because it can be so condensed – appeal to you for your IO, or would you choose another genre? Think about your reasoning.

TIP

Lars has highlighted phrases from the extract to use in his practice IO.

Here is Lars's chosen extract from William Wordsworth's 'The Prelude', with his annotations.

One summer evening (led by her) I found
A little boat tied to a willow tree
Within a rocky cove, its usual home.
Straight I unloosed her chain, and stepping in
Pushed from the shore. It was an act of stealth
And troubled pleasure, nor without the voice
Of mountain-echoes did my boat move on;
Leaving behind her still, on either side,
Small circles glittering idly in the moon,
Until they melted all into one track
Of sparkling light. But now, like one who rows,
Proud of his skill, to reach a chosen point
With an unswerving line, I fixed my view
Upon the summit of a craggy ridge,
The horizon's utmost boundary; far above
Was nothing but the stars and the grey sky.
She was an elfin pinnace; lustily
I dipped my oars into the silent lake,
And, as I rose upon the stroke, my boat
Went heaving through the water like a swan;
When, from behind that craggy steep till then
The horizon's bound, a huge peak, black and huge,

This could be mother nature

calm and beautiful

Simile of the swan: calm and control

Nature

Personification of nature

Panic
Repetition of 'struck and struck again'

Depresssion; maybe mankind was insignifiant

TIP

When annotating a text before your oral exam, this will be easier if the line spacing is wide. This creates more space for you to write ideas and helps you organise your thoughts.

As if with voluntary power instinct,
Upreared its head. I struck and struck again,
And growing still in stature the grim shape
Towered up between me and the stars, and still
For so it seemed, with purpose of its own
And measured motion like a living thing,
Strode after me. With trembling oars I turned,
And though the silent water stole my way
Back to the covert of the willow tree;
There in her mooring-place I left my bark, –
And through the meadows homeward went, in grave
And serious mood; but after I had seen
That spectacle, for many days, my brain
Worked with a dim and undetermined sense
Of unknown modes of being; o'er my thoughts
There hung a darkness, call it solitude
Or blank desertion. No familiar shapes
Remained, no pleasant images of trees,
Of sea or sky, no colours of green fields;
But huge and mighty forms, that do not live
Like living men, moved slowly through the mind
By day, and were a trouble to my dreams.

REFLECT

- What do you think of Lars's choice of literary text for the IO?
- How helpful would you find annotations such as these in your own IO?
- Is there anything you would add to Lars's annotations?
- How important do you think it is to annotate every line of an extract of this length?

TIP

Here is an extract from Lars's practice IO. You can find the full recording online and his original notes.

My first text is an extract from 'The Prelude' by William Wordsworth, and my second text is a speech made by Greta Thunberg, a 16-year-old climate activist who spoke at the UN climatic change conference on 15 December 2018. My global issue is human relationship to nature and how it has changed over time.

First I am going to start with 'The Prelude' by William Wordsworth that was published in 1750. The poem starts with the narrator being quite in control of the situation and he is going for a boat ride for pleasure. This can be seen in 'an active stealth and troubled pleasure'. So he is doing this for fun and when it gets to the middle of the poem, he sees this massive mountain and gets quite scared by it because he realises suddenly how insignificant he is in comparison to nature. This can be seen in 'huge peak, black and huge' and he also personifies this mountain in 'as if with voluntary power instinct'. So he feels that this mountain is almost alive and coming after him and he is quite scared by this because he has grown up in the industrial revolution where Christianity would have been the main religion, which teaches that humanity is above nature and that God has given nature to humans to use to better our quality of life. But that is not what William Wordsworth sees when he is rowing his boat. He is quite scared by this and this can be seen in 'with trembling oars'. So he changes direction and starts rowing back and he starts seeing this mountain almost come closer to him and when he gets back off the boat that image still stays with him so he is still trying to wrap his mind around how small he feels in comparison to nature and that goes against the ideas that he has grown up with. This can be seen in 'O'er my thoughts there hung a darkness', so he is quite troubled by the feeling of insignificance.

After doing the practice IO, Lars and his teacher reviewed his performance. His teacher commented that some of his phrases were imprecise, and suggested that, for his next practice IO, Lars should try to make his language more focused and formal. Lars's teacher picked out some examples of phrases he had used in this first section of his practice IO and suggested some alternatives.

ACTIVITY

Complete a copy of the following table by responding to the phrases in the context of this IO.

Original statement	Effect of the original	Suggested alternative statement	Effect of the suggested statement
'Quite in control of the situation'		'Seemingly in control of his fate'	
'He is doing this for fun'		'Wordsworth is embarking on this for pleasure'	
'When it gets to the middle of the poem'		'In line 13'	
'Massive mountain'		'Towering mountain'	
'Gets quite scared'		'Is overwhelmed'	
'He is still trying to get his mind around how small he feels'		'He is trying to comprehend how insignificant man is'	

REFLECT

How are the suggested statements more effective than the original text?

How does it change your impression of the speaker, and the tone of the analysis?

TIP

Whether you are doing an oral or a written assessment, you should always make sure that you express yourself formally. This means that you avoid using colloquial or casual language.

Informal English, or using an inappropriate register (such as 'gets quite scared' in this example) fails to convey meaning accurately, and does not represent you as someone who is taking the assessment seriously. The study of language and literature requires that you express your ideas with an appropriate level of sophistication and precision.

Text 2: language

Now look at the second part of Lars's IO. Here he brings in Greta Thunberg's speech at the COP24 climate change conference in 2018. It was a breakthrough moment for the young activist who suddenly found herself at the centre of global attention. Here is her speech, followed by Lars's commentary.

My name is Greta Thunberg. I am 15 years old. I am from Sweden. I speak on behalf of Climate Justice Now. Many people say that Sweden is just a small country and it doesn't matter what we do. But I've learned you are never too small to make a difference. And if a few children can get headlines all over the world just by not going to school, then imagine what we could all do together if we really wanted to.

But to do that, we have to speak clearly, no matter how uncomfortable that may be. You only speak of green eternal economic growth because you are too scared of being unpopular. You only talk about moving forward with the same bad ideas that got us into this mess, even when the only sensible thing to do is pull the emergency brake. You are not mature enough to tell it like it is. Even that burden you leave to us children. But I don't care about being popular. I care about climate justice and the living planet. Our civilization is being sacrificed for the opportunity of a very small number of people to continue making enormous amounts of money. Our biosphere is being sacrificed so that rich people in countries like mine can live in luxury. It is the sufferings of the many which pay for the luxuries of the few.

The year 2078, I will celebrate my 75th birthday. If I have children maybe they will spend that day with me. Maybe they will ask me about you. Maybe they will ask why you didn't do anything while there still was time to act. You say you love your children above all else, and yet you are stealing their future in front of their very eyes.

Until you start focusing on what needs to be done rather than what is politically possible, there is no hope. We can't solve a crisis without treating it as a crisis. We need to keep the fossil fuels in the ground, and we need to focus on equity. And if solutions within the system are so impossible to find, maybe we should change the system itself. We have not come here to beg world leaders to care. You have ignored us in the past and you will ignore us again. We have run out of excuses and we are running out of time. We have come here to let you know that change is coming, whether you like it or not. The real power belongs to the people. Thank you.

Greta Thunberg's speech at COP24, 2018

Here is Lars's response to this text. As you read it, annotate it and mark any sections that you think could gain, or lose, marks.

Moving on to the second text, a speech by Greta Thunberg. She uses quite simple vocabulary and a lot of collective pronouns – for example, 'we', 'our'. I feel this makes her speech quite powerful as she is being very inclusive with her speech so that makes it very hard to disagree with because she is saying that I am doing this for the benefit of everybody not just herself. So the use of simple language makes her speech quite powerful because she is being very direct. She is not using very eloquent vocabulary to show her meaning, she is being quite blunt with it. She is like 'This is what we need to do, why aren't we doing it?' I think that is the main aim of what she wants, she wants to be quite clear with people because people have been talking about climate change for a long time and nothing has happened about it. So she feels that someone just needs to be there to make it very clear, to make it very blunt to everyone just what needs to happen. A nice line that she says is 'You say you love your children above all else and yet you are stealing their future in front of their very eyes.' The verb 'stealing' is very powerful. It connotes crime and shows that she feels that what we are doing at the moment is a crime against humanity, how we are just trashing the biosphere and it gives a sense of urgency and a sense that climate change is a real problem and that we really need to face it now because we are in the last couple of years where we actually can.

Another quite interesting thing is that she repeats the word 'luxury' a lot. She sees our life that we are living at the moment as a luxury and that is it not beneficial and that we need to change the way we live because it is not helping our world, it is not helping the earth. She also says that 'the luxury of the few is built on the suffering of the many' and that we as developed countries will drastically need to change our way of life and our way of consumerism in order to give less developed countries a chance to become more developed and have a better quality of life. She repeats the word 'sacrifice' quite a bit. She is saying that our civilisation is being sacrificed for money and being sacrificed so that rich people can have luxury and money and that this is not right, this is short-sighted and idiotic and we need to wake up and change this because this is not going to better our lives, it is just going to better a few people's lives for maybe one or two generations and then it is all lost.

Peer-assessment

Write down your first impressions of Lars's analysis of Thunberg's speech. How effective is it? How could it have been improved?

Here is Lars's conclusion to his practice IO:

The main theme for each literary text is different. So the Prelude by William Wordsworth is about feeling insignificant, small and powerless compared to the enormity of nature but Greta Thunberg's speech is almost about the opposite – it is about how we have become too powerful and too short-sighted and that we have started destroying our planet. I think it is quite interesting how our perspectives on nature have changed so drastically in the past 170 or so years. So we have gone from fearing and respecting nature and not being able to do anything about it to having the technology and the short-sightedness and greed to nearly destroy it. Both texts have fear as a main theme throughout. Greta Thunberg's fear is that we won't act on climate change on time and make a difference. This can be seen in 'you have ignored us in the past and you will ignore us again'. So she is acknowledging that we are going to be ignored and she feels that the only way that anything is going to be done is through a revolution. Wordsworth's fear is the feeling of insignificance towards himself in comparison to nature and the earth and how large that is because he has been brought up in a society that constantly tells him that he and humanity are greater than nature and the natural world and he realises in this extract from the Prelude that that is not the case and it kind of throws him into a depression, which can be seen in 'O'er my thoughts there hung a darkness', so he is still trying to wrap his head around how small he really is in comparison to everything else.

Now read the discussion between Lars and his teacher after his practice IO.

Teacher: *Thank you. How do you think that humans' relationship to nature has changed in the time when Wordsworth was writing to the time of Greta Thunberg's speech and how is that reflected in the texts?*

Lars: *In William Wordsworth's time, nature was still quite prevalent and we had only just started the industrial revolution and most of England was still quite rural and this can be seen in the act of him rowing on a lake at night, which was quite normal, whereas in Greta Thunberg's speech that is not something that her generation could do because a lot of it has been destroyed, so much so that it is worrying how little we have left.*

Teacher: *The language that they both use describes nature but they use quite different language to do that. How does that language contrast?*

Lars: *William Wordsworth describes nature as something very large, something that he could barely wrap his mind around and something that he was quite scared of because of how powerful it was, whereas Greta Thunberg is talking about, in her speech, how we are sacrificing our biosphere for monetary gain and she is quite worried about how little nature we have left and how quickly we are destroying it for something as virtual as money. The word 'biosphere' is quite interesting in the way she uses it. Biosphere would mean that we are all in a circle, we are all equal and nothing is above the other and if something dies, it affects everything else in the biosphere. So she is not thinking that humanity is above nature but rather that we are part of it, as a part of a whole rather than above it.*

Teacher: *What are the points of commonality that Wordsworth and Greta Thunberg share in their language around nature?*

Lars: *Both of them have a great love for nature. In the beginning of the Prelude, Wordsworth uses a line, for example, 'small circles glittering idly in the moon', which shows a calm and beautiful idea of what nature is, and Greta sees nature as a necessity – we need it to stay alive and it is beautiful and she wants future generations to be able to experience the same thing. She says 'In the year 2078 I'll celebrate my 75th birthday. If I have children, maybe they will spend that day with me, maybe they will ask me about you, maybe they will ask why you didn't do anything.' She really wants that her children and her grandchildren can experience nature and can experience the beauty of it and it is unfair if we rob it from them.*

Teacher: *If you imagine the voice of Wordsworth and the voice of Thunberg as they come across in these extracts, what do you think they would have to say to each other if they were to meet now?*

> **Lars:** *I think they both come at the idea of nature from two very different perspectives. Williams Wordsworth comes from the perspective of feeling like he is greater and mightier than nature and then gets put in his place almost when he sees this massive mountain that is so much greater than he is. Greta sees us as a part of nature already, so she already has an almost more mature view than Wordsworth. I think what they would say to each other is that Greta would have a lot to say, she would be saying that we are part of it we are not above it and I think that William would be saying the same thing.*
>
> **Teacher:** *So they would meet and agree. Thank you.*

You can find a recording of Lars's practice IO online on Cambridge GO. Here is Lars's teacher's grading of his practice IO.

Criterion A	Knowledge, understanding and interpretation	There is **some** knowledge and understanding of the extracts, but it is uneven. The analysis of the Wordsworth extract is relatively weak, and the links made with the global issue are not well argued. The student did better with Text 2, and was stronger on the language used. The interpretation of both texts is insecure and the references to Wordsworth's language are infrequent and often not convincing.
Criterion B	Analysis and evaluation	The oral contains **some** relevant analysis but is mostly descriptive. Some authorial choices are identified and analysed, but this is less frequent in the Wordsworth extract than the Thunberg.
Criterion C	Focus and organisation	There is **some** focus on the task, but the treatment of both texts is uneven. The student was more confident with Thunberg's text and the issues raised than the Wordsworth extract. Points made in both lack real coherence.
Criterion D	Language	The language is not always clear and accurate, and for the Wordsworth extract there is an inexactness which obscures real meaning. Errors are in evidence, both in what is said and in how it is expressed. Register and tone are sometimes inappropriate.

The final marks awarded to Lars by his teacher for his practice IO were:

Criterion A:	3
Criterion B:	3
Criterion C:	3
Criterion D:	3
	12/40

REFLECT

Do you think the mark awarded to Lars is fair?

- What advice would you give Lars for his next practice IO?
- Should he choose different texts?
- If he does, what approach would you suggest he takes to improve his marks?

Write a ten-point plan for Lars's IO that is clearly focused on improving his response.

After reflecting on Lars's practice IO, and discussing it with a partner, how would you grade his performance? Base your marks on the assessment criteria.

Sample individual oral 3

Tory is studying English language and literature HL. She is interested in the literature of displaced people, and the political forces that shape the modern world. The two texts she has chosen for her individual oral are an extract from 'Twenty Six Malignant Gates', the second part of the novel *The Joy Luck Club* by Amy Tan, and an interview with Amy Chua, author of *The Battle Hymn of the Tiger Mother*.

Global issue	How is the Chinese diaspora issue represented?
Thesis statement	Both texts discuss the representation of mother–daughter relationships within the Chinese diasporic experience, particularly within the United States.
Guiding question	How similar are the experiences described by the writers in relation to the Chinese–American experience?
What stylistic features or devices from the first text are relevant to the global issue?	Focus on key themes in Text 1
What stylistic features or devices from the second text are relevant to the global issue?	Focus on key themes in Text 2
Prompt	Examine the ways in which the global issue of your choice is presented through the content and form of two of the texts you have studied.

Text 1: language

Here is the extract from the interview with Amy Chua:

KEY CONCEPT

Community

Community can be a fascinating 'lens' with which to view literary and non-literary texts. Wherever people from the same cultures congregate, they create new and different communities, sometimes sharing lived experiences and cultures, and sometimes seeking to protect them from being lost.

At its heart, Battle Hymn is an account of the psychological warfare between a 'Chinese' mother and her 'western' daughter and in telling it, Chua raises an interesting set of questions about bringing up children, cultural norms and the confessional mode: namely, why expose herself? Why choose to open her mouth at all? At what point does confessing in print that you called your child 'garbage' to her face cease to be a comment on Chinese parenting and resume its traditional function as a sign that you are two cards short of a deck?

Chua, 46, is a professor of law at Yale Law School who writes critically acclaimed books on free-market democracy and global instability. Her husband, Jed Rubenfeld, 51, also a law professor at Yale (they met as students at Harvard Law School), is a well-known Jewish–American academic. On the morning I meet her, on a freezing day in New York, she has travelled into Manhattan by train from New Haven, Connecticut, where the family lives.

Sitting opposite me sipping water in Norwood, an arts club in Chelsea, in a black sweater and miniskirt with silver hoops in her ears, she is petite and pretty and much softer looking than in her book-jacket photograph ('She doesn't *look* very mean,' my son said.) If on the page she can come across as a little unhinged, in person she is charming, warm, down to earth, and quick to laugh. The truth is, we are definitely in a monster-free zone.

'I think I know what's to come,' Chua says with a wry smile. 'When I show this book to immigrants and immigrants' kids, they were like, exactly, this is how it is. It's funny, they relate, it's not controversial for them. Now among my western friends it provokes extremely intense reactions in all directions. Some, including my closest friends, are shocked and aghast.' Did she anticipate this reaction? 'I do now. My husband kept warning me and my sisters kept warning me. But I guess it's part of my personality. A little bit rash. For me, so much of my book is making fun of myself through the words of my children. And some people get that. Other people read it straight. My older daughter said, "Mummy, you put only the most extreme stories in. People don't realise how much fun we had".'

What Chua didn't put in the memoir, she says with a hint of regret, is all the good times. 'All the way through, Jed was bringing balance to the family, insisting that we were going to go on family bike rides and to Yankees games and apple-picking and water slides and bowling and mini-golfing, so we socialised a lot actually …' ('My mum has a touch of the dramatic, and she's much nicer in real life,' Sophia says to me later by email. 'She lets me go to rap concerts with my friends and do archaeological digs in our backyard – not very 'Chinese' activities!')

She'd had no idea that she was going to write her testimonial to 'Chinese' mothering and its dangers, but in the black, bleak summer of 2009 that followed her beloved sister Katrin's diagnosis of leukaemia, when her 13-year-old daughter Lulu was in full rebellion, she began to put pen to paper. 'I wrote this in a moment of crisis. I tend to be over-confident but I really felt that the whole family was falling apart, I thought, have I done every single thing wrong? Have I wrecked everything? So after one terrible blow-up [with Lulu], I got on my computer and the words just poured out.'

Over a period of two months she wrote, revised, edited, all the while consulting Jed, Sophia and Lulu, showing them 'every single page', she says proudly. 'It was like family therapy.' When she had finished the remembering, she showed it to her parents and close friends, all of whom told her not to publish. '[They] said, "Oh you're going to get in such trouble, you can't talk about this in the west." And that kind of got my back up. I thought, why should we not be able to talk about this? It's not just me. Millions of people raise their kids this way and their kids come out pretty well.'

Extract from the interview with Amy Chua, *The Guardian*, 15 January 2011

You can find a copy of Tory's handwritten notes for her IO online on Cambridge GO.

REFLECT

- What do you think of this choice of text for an IO?
- Do you think the language used, and the ideas explored in this interview, offer enough depth for an IO?
- How would you annotate this extract in preparation for the IO? What words or phrases would you focus on?

AREAS OF EXPLORATION

Connecting texts

Throughout the English A: Language and Literature course, you should be looking at ways of connecting works. Finding patterns that connect writers and texts deepens your knowledge and understanding of all forms of communication. When you see obvious common themes between texts, make a note of these in your learner portfolio. Over time, and with practice, the links you have made will become easier to talk and write about, and this will benefit you in other assessments in your course.

TIP

Every student has a different way of taking notes. Make sure, when you start writing yours, that they work for you, and are clear and well structured. In IOs, students can often be distracted by unclear notes, leading them to make points that move away from the subject and do not address the prompt.

Here is a transcript of Tory's practice IO. Her teacher made some brief comments as Tory was speaking.

Good start: texts clearly linked

> The two texts I am doing is an extract from the chapter called 'Twenty-six malignant gates' in the novel *The Joy Luck Club* by Amy Tan and the other text I am doing is an extract from an interview with Amy Chua, who is the author of a parenting memoir called *The Battle Hymn of the Tiger Mother*. I am linking these two texts to the global issue of how is the Chinese migrant diaspora experience represented.

Good explanation further explaining links between the texts; some slips in expression

> *The Joy Luck Club* was a novel written in 1989 and it tells the story of four mother–daughter immigrant families who live in the US. The second interview extract is regarding the parenting memoir that Amy Chua wrote. When she published this book there was a lot of controversy surrounding what she had written about her parenting methods as she took pride in her role as a 'tiger mother', a term usually culturally describing an Asian mother who is very strict in her parenting, and she was responding to the backlash by saying that she wasn't the monster that she represented herself to be. And so I felt like both texts discussed the representation of mother–daughter relationships within the Chinese diasporic experience, particularly within the United States there is cultural dissonant both described but also I think the whitewashing of Asian voices as well.

Interesting extension of analysis by bringing in Said's text. How valid is this?

> *The Joy Luck Club* is presented as storytelling of the Chinese migrant culture and in the extract in particular it's about an argument between a mother and her daughter and how the daughter is upset because she felt like her mother is being too strict on her about piano practice. I analysed this through Edward Said's theory of Orientalism, which states that the dominant Western culture 'Others' other ethnic cultures by asserting that they are different from themselves.

> I felt that this was also applicable to the first-generation and second-generation migrant experience where the daughter uses the language 'I wasn't her slave. This wasn't China' and 'Others' herself from her mother by claiming her identity was a rejection of her mother's Chinese migrant parenting and further her Chinese values and her parenting. And so the chapter title itself, 'Twenty-six malignant gates', is a reference to a Chinese text referring to the fact that a mother has to watch over her daughter because bad things will happen to her if she looks away.

Good analysis, and makes it contemporary; focuses on identity

> Amy Tan narrates the voice of the Chinese mother as almost a production of this oppressive, exoticised Chinese culture where she is vulnerable and backwards and this is where I think that the controversy of the book, where the critics said that it was reinforcing stereotypes of the Chinese mother, was coming in to, as the mother was described as 'her mouth was open, smiling crazily as she was pleased that I was praying'. And the mother says oppressive language such as 'Only one kind of daughter can live in this household. Obedient daughter', in which the punctuation of the two words 'Obedient daughter' is emphasised. And I felt as if this language instead of representing

what the parenting values of Asian culture could be, was instead presenting the mother as devilling to the daughter who represented the merger of Western and Chinese culture, so further representing the migrant mother as the carrier of a culture that's backwards. So the mother is not only presented as devilling but she is also a victim in her own text as later on the daughter makes a remark that really hurts the mother and says 'as if she were blowing away like a small brown leaf, thin, brittle, and lifeless'. This again is emphasised with commas between the words 'thin', 'brittle' and 'lifeless', emphasising that she is a victim of her own culture and I thought that this is again a rejection of Chinese culture through the Chinese migrant experience as the exposure to Western culture is victimising herself and she becomes a victim of her own culture.

> Very good, close focus on language, and punctuation, and in doing so draws out some of the extracts key themes

Peer-assessment

How would you assess the first part of Tory's practice IO? Is it stronger than Zeynep's and Lars's practice IOs? Support your views with evidence from the text above.

Now look at the criteria: which mark band do you think Tory would be likely to achieve for each of the criteria?

Criteria	Level descriptors (with key words)	What mark band would you put Tory in at this stage of her IO?
A: Knowledge, understanding and interpretation	1–2 'little knowledge' 3–4 'some knowledge' 5–6 'satisfactory knowledge' 7–8 'good knowledge' 9–10 'excellent knowledge'	
B: Analysis and evaluation	1–2 'descriptive' 3–4 'some relevant analysis' 5–6 'analytical in nature' 7–8 'at times insightful' 9–10 'thorough and nuanced'	
C: Focus and organisation	1–2 'rarely focuses on task' 3–4 'sometimes focuses on task' 5–6 'maintains a focus' 7–8 'mostly clear and sustained focus' 9–10 'maintains a clear and sustained focus'	

Criteria	Level descriptors (with key words)	What mark band would you put Tory in at this stage of her IO?
D: Language	1–2 'rarely clear' 3–4 'generally clear' 5–6 'clear' 7–8 'clear and accurate' 9–10 'clear, accurate and varied'	

Here is a transcript of the second part of Tory's IO, with the teacher's comments:

Should the link between the two be stronger and not such a contrast?

This is in contrast to *The Battle Hymn of the Tiger Mother* as in the interview the representation of Amy Chua is completely different. Amy Chua, unlike the representation of Suyuan, who is the mother in *The Joy Luck Club*, is presented as successful, modern and an intellectual. The interview describes her role, and the news article featuring the interview describes her as charming, warm, down to earth, quick to laugh, which almost seems to be reassuring the readers that she is not the monster that she presented herself to be in her novel and that she is human – it is humanising her.

Some very interesting points about reclaiming identity, but some slips in Criterion D: Language

Also the article uses humour with parenthesis such as, although she is described to be charming, warm and down to earth, when the writer says '(my son didn't think she was like a monster at all)' and it almost feels as if Amy Chua reclaimed her own narrative by writing her story as a tiger mother. As then again her voice is being oppressed by the Western gaze as it almost felt as if the article was saying that 'Oh, actually she is not the powerful Asian mother she wrote herself to be as she is described to be wearing a black sweater, earrings and a skirt at an uptown restaurant in Chelsea, New York.' She is not the typical exoticised image we have of Asian mothers in ethnic clothing speaking in Mandarin. So not only is she introduced to be a Western migrant who is humanised from her own work, the image of herself she presents in her interview seems to be taken away by the language surrounding her clothes.

Sophisticated analysis: Criterion B: analysis and evaluation, but again some slips in D

In the interview she says that her Asian friends discouraged her from publishing the book. She says 'Oh, I responded to "You can't talk about this in the West" with I thought "Why shouldn't we be able to talk about this?"' and the sentence following her claim that she wanted to reclaim her story as a tiger mother was her husband stated that she actually had a lot of freedom. They went apple-picking. And then again I thought this was erasure of her narrative by constantly reassuring the reader that she wasn't the monster tiger mother that the article seems to be undermining her as. So there appears to be a contradiction of her representation in the article as the article simultaneously claims her to be powerful for telling her narrative of the tiger mother but also simultaneously using a Westernised lens and not truly narrating her story.

Therefore, I felt as if these two representations of these two Chinese migrant mothers were not truly represented in their own authentic voices as the first one presented the Asian mother to be trapped within her own oppressive culture. In the context of the novel being published, Amy Tan's books received a lot of well-acclaimed appraisal as people felt as if for the first time Asian voices were truly being represented in popular culture but at the same time she did not truly narrate the story as it was as if she was narrating the story of an Asian migrant from a hegemony of Western culture, almost as if she was binding herself to typical Western stereotypes of the Asian migrant. And this again is seen through her only of being the ignorant mother who is not aware of the liberal Western parenting methods but also through the language she has described to use where short sentences also seem to mimic poorly spoken English and in *The Battle Hymn of the Tiger Mother* and in this interview, you would think that in her original book she was reclaiming the role of the tiger mom as she was retelling a typically Western narrated role through her own experiences. But then again through this extract she is seen to be a victim of the Western lens where it is almost like the author is making fun of her with his use of humour and the whole 'Oh she's not a monster because she is down to earth and she is funny' and it is problematic because it's also erasure of her voice. Therefore I felt as if the Chinese migrant diasporic experience represented in Western culture ultimately binds voices to a Western hegemony where certain stereotypes are continually perpetrated such as the strict mother, the vulnerable migrant mother who are unaware of Western culture and this linking back to Edward Said's Orientalism is again, showing that Western culture is superior over other cultures because they are different and when they are put in a Western culture they are the vulnerable ignorant ones.

You can find a copy of the discussion between Tory and her teacher, which completed her IO, online on Cambridge GO.

Here is Tory's teacher's assessment of her practice IO.

Criterion A	Knowledge, understanding and interpretation	There is excellent knowledge and understanding of the extracts. The global issue is explored effectively.
Criterion B	Analysis and evaluation	At times insightful, this is a persuasive evaluation of these two extracts. There is a nuanced understanding of both texts, but in particular the Chua interview.
Criterion C	Focus and organisation	Very good structure: well introduced, developed and linked. Clear and sustained and on task, the development of ideas is strong and valid. Persuasive and clear.
Criterion D	Language	The language is clear and accurate; vocabulary choices are almost always excellent. Register is appropriate and enhances the individual oral. The answers to the questions are very good.

Peer-assessment

After reflecting on Tory's practice IO, and what you have discussed with a partner, how would you grade her performance? Base your marks on the assessment criteria.

The final marks awarded to Tory by her teacher were:

Criterion A:	9
Criterion B:	9
Criterion C:	9
Criterion D:	9
	36/40

REFLECT

Do you think the mark awarded to Tory is fair?

- What advice would you give Tory for her next practice IO?
- Should she choose different texts?
- If she does, what approach would you suggest she takes to improve her marks?

Write a ten-point plan for Tory's IO which is clearly focused on improving her response.

Recording of four different students' IOs, together with their notes, are available online on Cambridge GO.

OVER TO YOU

Many of us are uncomfortable hearing our own voices; some of us are surprised by how many times we use 'fillers' such as 'like' and 'kind of', or hesitations such as 'uh' or 'er'. These are perfectly natural and normal parts of conversational speech, but when we are in a formal situation we can become more self-conscious of how often we use them.

Try recording yourself speaking about simple tasks, such as describing a picture or discussing a poem. Ask a classmate to give you feedback on what they hear, perhaps asking them to focus on one aspect that you think could be improved (such as fillers, or the pace of your delivery).

You could self-assess your performance: record yourself presenting a spoken analysis on two different texts for the IO, and use the criteria to grade your presentation.

All this takes very little time and, with practice, can help in developing both the skills and the self-confidence to do well in the IO.

Practice papers

In this section you will:

- answer example exam-style questions for Paper 1 and Paper 2
- write exam-style essays under timed conditions.

Paper 1

Your Paper 1 examination will include *two* non-literary texts. If you are an SL student, you should write about *one* of the texts. That is, you have a choice of which text you write about. If you are an HL student, you must write about *both* texts. That is, you have no choice of which text you write about.

If you are an HL student, and have to write about both texts, it is important to allow roughly the same amount of time to write about each text. If you are an SL student, and have to write about only one text, use the 5 minutes' reading time that precedes your examination to begin to make your selection. Be certain about which text you intend to write about and do not change your mind.

Each Paper 1 examination paper will ask you to write an analysis of *one* of the texts (at SL) or *both* of the texts (at HL). Also, you will be told that you do *not* have to address the guiding question that accompanies each text. While you need not address the guiding question, you must still write an analysis that is focused. By addressing the guiding question, you ensure that your analysis is focused. It is best to establish focus by directly responding to the guiding question, as it provides you with a main argument to develop.

Here are two sample examination papers. These are typical of the type of question you may encounter in the Paper 1 exam. Try practising for your examination by writing a response to each of the texts. You may find it useful practice to write your response under timed conditions.

Paper 1: practice paper 1

Text A

Join the school strike for climate

Some things are worth breaking the rules for.

In towns and cities all over the world, millions of students are marching for their future and demanding immediate action to address the global climate crisis. Now the youth have called on the rest of us to join them! There are thousands of events. Are you in?

<u>Students can't wait to lead</u>

Our house is on fire – let's act like it. If nothing gets done in the next ten years, we'll be coming of age in a world where salvaging a liveable climate is close to impossible. That's how late it is, and how little our 'leaders' have led. When you're not doing everything we can to secure a world we can thrive in for generations, why on Earth should we sit in school? That's why we're taking to the streets.

> The world needs to listen
>
> In the space of a year, school children on every continent have organised themselves to demand climate action for our shared future. We are done waiting for the politicians who have failed to act our entire lives. Now we've stopped playing by the rules and we've started to move. Everything may be about to change, because for us it has to.
>
> From the Greenpeace webpage (2019)

Discuss how different features are used in this webpage to persuade the reader to take action.

Text B

> The Elixir of Life–In a Poisoned Chalice?
>
> by George Monbiot
>
> Is life extension science an astonishing promise or an astonishing threat? Or both?
>
> It was once a myth, now it's dream; soon it will become an expectation. Suddenly the science of life extension is producing some remarkable results. New papers hint at the possibility of treatments that could radically increase human longevity[1,2,3,4].
>
> So much is happening that it's hard to know where to begin. But I'll pick just two of the gathering developments. The first concerns a class of enzymes called sirtuins. This month's Trends in Genetics states that the question of whether these enzymes could increase longevity in mammals "has now been settled decidedly in the affirmative"[5].
>
> Last month a new paper in the journal Aging Cell showed how synthetic small molecules (in other words, potential drugs) can stimulate the production of sirtuins in mice[6]. This both extends their lifespan and improves their health. These results show, the paper says, that it's "possible to design a small molecule that can slow aging and delay multiple age-related diseases in mammals, supporting the therapeutic potential … in humans."

1   See for example (among thousands of possibilities): Alexey A Moskalev et al, June 2014. Genetics and epigenetics of aging and longevity. Cell Cycle 13:7, 1063–1077. http://dx.doi.org/10.4161/cc.28433

2   Akiko Satoh and Shin-ichiro Imai, 26 June 2014. Systemic regulation of mammalian ageing and longevity by brain sirtuins. Nature Communications, 5, #4211. doi:10.1038/ncomms5211. http://www.nature.com/ncomms/2014/140626/ncomms5211/full/ncomms5211.html

3   Dena B. Dubal et al, May 2014. Life Extension Factor Klotho Enhances Cognition. Cell Reports, Volume 7, Issue 4, p1065–1076. http://dx.doi.org/10.1016/j.celrep.2014.03.076

4   http://www.digitalafro.com/real-fountain-of-youth-scientists-able-to-turn-off-the-aging-gene-in-mice/

5   William Giblin, Mary E. Skinner, and David B. Lombard, July 2014. Sirtuins: guardians of mammalian healthspan. Trends in Genetics, Vol. 30, No. 7, pp271–286. doi: 10.1016/j.tig.2014.04.007

5

The second development I've plucked from the tumult of extraordinary new science concerns an external hormone (a pheromone) secreted by nematode worms, called daumone. A new paper reports that when daumone is fed to elderly mice, it reduced the risk of death by 48% across five months[7]. "Daumone could be developed as an anti-aging compound."

There are still plenty of missing steps, not least clinical trials and drug development, but there's a strong sense that we stand at an extraordinary moment.

Who would not want this? To cheat the gods and mock the reaper? The benefits are so obvious that one recent article insists political leaders who fail to provide sufficient funding for life extension science should be charged with manslaughter[8]. It's thrilling, dazzling, awe-inspiring. And rather alarming.

The most visible champion of life extension science, Aubrey de Grey, contends that "a lot of people alive today are going to live to 1,000 or more". He lists four common concerns, that he rejects as "unbelievable excuses … for aging", "ridiculous" and "completely crazy, when you actually remember your sense of proportion."[9] On the first count – "wouldn't it be crushingly boring?" – he's right. Life, if you have a degree of economic choice, is as exciting as we choose to make it. If it becomes too dull, well, you can just stop taking your medicine.

The other concerns are not so easily dismissed. "How would we pay the pensions?" is the second question he ridicules. I would rephrase it: "how would the very old support themselves without crushing the young?". Even today, there are major distributional problems in countries like the UK. Wealthy elderly people, enjoying the compound interest from investments accumulated across decades, preside over a rentier economy that's devastating to the young and poor, as house prices and rents become unaffordable[10]. The inequality and the potential for exploitation that would emerge if people lived twice, not to mention ten times, as long can only be boggled at.

This takes us to another concern he dismisses: "dictators would rule forever". Is this proposition (if not taken literally) ridiculous? They hang on long enough already, with the help of the best healthcare their stolen billions can buy. Match the political power longevity offers with the economic power, and it's not impossible to see how a thousand-year life could lead to a thousand-year reich.

---

6   Evi M. Mercken et al, 16 June 2014. SRT2104 extends survival of male mice on a standard diet and preserves bone and muscle mass. Aging Cell, doi: 10.1111/acel.12220. http://onlinelibrary.wiley.com/doi/10.1111/acel.12220/pdf

7   Jong Hee Park, 6th May 2014. Daumone fed late in life improves survival and reduces hepatic inflammation and fibrosis in mice. Aging Cell, doi: 10.1111/acel.12224

8   http://www.psychologytoday.com/blog/the-transhumanist-philosopher/201401/when-does-hindering-life-extension-science-become-crime

9   http://www.ted.com/talks/aubrey_de_grey_says_we_can_avoid_aging#t-174230

10   http://www.theguardian.com/commentisfree/2014/jun/02/housing-tax-property-help-to-buy-government-schemes

de Grey's mockery becomes most offensive when invoked by his fourth rhetorical question: "what about starving Africans?". Yes, what about them? What if, beyond a certain point, longevity becomes a zero-sum game? What if every year of life extension for those who can afford the treatment becomes a year or more of life reduction for those who can't?

Already, on this planet of finite resources, rich and poor are locked into unacknowledged conflict, as hyperconsumption reduces the planet's capacity to sustain life. Grain is used to produce meat rather than feeding people directly; the safe operating space for humanity is narrowed by greenhouse gases, industrial pollutants, freshwater depletion and soil erosion[11]. It's hard, after a while, to see how this could produce any outcome other than a direct competition for the means of life, which some must win and others must lose. Perhaps the rich must die so that the poor can live.

It's true that the price of possible longevity treatments, which will be astronomical at first, would soon start to plummet. But this is a world in which many can't afford even antiseptic ointment; a world in which, even in the rich countries, universal access to healthcare is being slowly throttled by a selfish elite; in which a new era of personalised medicine coincides, by unhappy accident, with a new era of crushing inequality. The idea that everyone would soon have access to these therapies looks unfeasible. It's possible, as an article in Aeon magazine speculates[12], that two classes of people – the treated and the untreated – could pull inexorably apart, the first living ever longer, the second dying even younger than they do today.

I don't know the answers to these questions, and I'm far from being able to propose solutions. It's all unknown from now on. But I do know that it's foolish to dismiss them.

Life extension science could invoke a sunlit, miraculous world of freedom from fear and long-term thinking. Or a gerontocratic tyranny. If it's the latter, I hope I don't live long enough to see it.

Published in The Guardian, 8 July 2014

In what ways does the writer use language to express his views on the science of life extension?

11 See http://www.kateraworth.com/doughnut/

12 http://aeon.co/magazine/being-human/will-new-drugs-mean-the-rich-live-to-120-and-the-poor-die-at-60/

Paper 1: practice paper 2

Text A

Crazy Rich Asians Review

When Nick (Henry Golding) invites his girlfriend Rachel (Constance Wu) to a wedding in Singapore, she sees it as a chance to meet his family and find out where he came from. On arrival, Rachel learns Nick has been keeping a little secret: they're the richest people in the country.

By Olly Richards. Posted 29 Aug 2018

Release Date: 13 Sep 2018

You cannot for a second accuse *Crazy Rich Asians* of failing to deliver on its title. Almost every one of its characters has a fat bank account and is not afraid to show it, as gaudily and fabulously as they possibly can. That title, larky and campy as it is, is something else, too. It's a statement. The past five years or so have seen studios finally pulling their finger out when it comes to putting money behind movies with casts that are predominantly non-white and there has been a lot of focus on the success of movies with largely black casts — *Black Panther*, *Girls Trip*, *Straight Outta Compton*, etc. *Crazy Rich Asians* is a statement that diversity means a whole range of ethnicities and experiences, and everyone should be included. It clearly knows it's important, as the first major studio movie of the century with an Asian cast, but it wears that importance lightly, and festooned in sequins. It is a hoot, subtly very clever, and one of the best romantic-comedies of the decade.

At the centre of an enormous cast are Constance Wu and Henry Golding as Rachel and Nick, a young, attractive couple living in New York, where both work as professors at NYU. Things are getting serious and when Nick is due to go to Singapore, where his best friend is getting married, he asks Rachel to come along. Rachel knows most of Nick's family is in Singapore. What she does not realise, until they arrive, is that Nick's family owns most of Singapore. He is the heir to the fortune of a real estate dynasty and something of a national celebrity. As Rachel is introduced to his enormous extended family she learns that many people don't want to let the country's most eligible bachelor go to some interloper American. Unfortunately, that group includes Nick's mother, Eleanor (Michelle Yeoh).

Director Jon M. Chu's CV is an erratic list, taking in two *Step Up* movies, two Justin Bieber concert films, the *G.I. Joe* sequel and *Now You See Me 2*. What all those movies have in common is a good amount of dazzle, and he brings that here. Whether it's a wedding of such ludicrous grandiosity that the aisle is turned into a babbling brook before the bride makes her (confusingly damp) entrance, or a family party that resembles a royal gala, he revels in the opulence of his characters' rarefied lives. And while the past works of cinematographer Vanja Cernjul don't show anything comparably glossy, he does the movie proud. You never suspect these Asians are merely moderately well off.

What Chu also shows, better than he ever has before, is control of character. Initially the film is jolly and sweet, with jokes that raise a smile if not an out-loud laugh, but it gets more charming and funnier as the characters bed in and their real insecurities beneath their expensive surface start to show through. Rachel, superbly played by Wu, comes through particularly strongly, a woman who is out of her element but quick to adapt. It manages to make her dismay about dating a secret billionaire genuinely sympathetic.

It's common in films with so many players for things to become jumbled, for characters to feel included to just add another 'name' to the cast, but Chu knits them all together fluently. The supporting cast is full of great turns, particularly Gemma Chan as a millionaire with an insecure husband, and Michelle Yeoh. Leaving them all for dust, though, is Awkwafina, as Rachel's best friend Goh Peik Lin, who looks like an illustration of the Dolly Parton quote, "It takes a lot of money to look this cheap." Despite being in her twenties, she has the qualities of someone like Joan Rivers body-swapped with a trust-funded millennial.

Amid all the laughter, Peter Chiarelli and Adele Lim's adaptation of Kevin Kwan's 2013 novel works in some interesting conversations about the changes in Asian culture as it has travelled around the world. The film is fantastical, but it has a lot of real-world points to make and feels like a discussion that's only just getting started. A sequel is already in the works, and it can't come soon enough.

From the *Empire* magazine webpage www.empireonline.com (2018)

Discuss the different ways in which this text simultaneously expresses an opinion and entertains its reader.

Text B

Photograph taken by Spencer Platt (2006)

How do different elements in this image combine to create a sense of narrative?

5

Paper 2

Paper 2 examinations are taken at the end of your course, in either May or November.

Paper 2 examinations are identical for HL and SL students. Papers contain *four* questions. You should answer *one* only, basing your answer on *two* literary works you have studied. You are *not* permitted to bring copies of works you have studied into the examination room.

Here are two sample examination papers. These are typical of the type of question you may encounter in the Paper 2 exam. Try practising for your examination by writing a response to each of the questions. You may find it useful practice to write your response under timed conditions.

Paper 2: practice paper 1

Answer *one* essay question only. You must base your answer on *two* of the works you have studied, and compare and contrast these works in response to the question.

1. We sometimes make a distinction between non-literary texts and literary works. Referring to two of the works you have studied, discuss some of the ways that the works can be considered literary.

2. Literary works sometimes show men and women in conflict with one another. To what extent is this true in two of the works you have studied?

3. 'Only I can change my life. No one can do it for me.' Discuss how characters in two of the works you have studied have overcome challenges to change their lives.

4. In two works you have studied, how do authorial choices regarding setting (period and place) influence the lives of characters?

Paper 2: practice paper 2

Answer *one* essay question only. You must base your answer on *two* of the works you have studied, and compare and contrast these works in response to the question.

1. In reference to two of the works you have studied, analyse the techniques used by writers to evoke a sense of tension.

2. Discuss the impact of death and dying in two of the works you have studied.

3. To what extent can two of the works you have studied be regarded as works of protest?

4. Referring to two literary works you have studied, compare and contrast characters who are alienated. In each of these works, what is the relationship between alienated characters and their setting?

Sample HL essays and assessment criteria

In this section you will:

- find example HL essays with teacher comments
- find assessment criteria for Paper 1, Paper 2 and the IO.

Sample HL essay 1

How does the television drama *Breaking Bad* conform to or deviate from the conventions of the 16th-century morality play?

At first glance, the American television drama *Breaking Bad* does not seem to bear much resemblance to the morality play, a form of vernacular drama from the 16th century. While both are intended to entertain, the primary purpose of the morality play was, by demonstrating the importance of good deeds, to encourage audiences to live virtuous, Catholic lives. *Breaking Bad*, sated with evil deeds, makes no equivalent endeavour to influence its audience. Instead, it shows a journey from good to evil.

On closer inspection, however, the television drama does evoke many of the conventions of the morality play. Both revolve around the actions of an everyman character who has the opportunity to demonstrate moral agency. And, both depict crime and punishment, and assign key virtues to specific characters.

The texts differ in their treatment of religious themes, such as the afterlife; the morality play was predicated on such typically Catholic beliefs, whereas Walter White, the protagonist in *Breaking Bad*, lacks any religious conviction. The texts also differ in the choices made by central characters. The medieval protagonists generally endeavoured to make righteous choices, while Walter finds fulfillment in his reprehensible choices. These differences emerge, no doubt in large part, from the contrasting cultural contexts of medieval Europe and contemporary America – one religious, the other secular.

Turning first to consider more fully the similarities between the morality play and the television drama, viewers notice from the incipiency of *Breaking Bad* that Walter is created as an everyman character. Although he is knowledgeable in chemistry – arguably his 'superpower' – he is otherwise ordinary, making him sympathetic to audiences. A high school teacher and his wife, Skyler, pregnant with their second child, Walter's financial difficulties correspond to the lived lives of many ordinary Americans. An underachiever who is overqualified for his profession, Walter's primary function is to undergo an immoral evolution. Indeed, it is Walter's unremarkable qualities that (initially) endear him to the viewer, and increase the authenticity of his loss of morality. If the transition from everyman is atypical of the morality play, it is nevertheless the case that the characters in *Breaking Bad* exist in a manifestly moral universe.

The notion of characters suffering the repercussions of their misdeeds is central to *Breaking Bad*, and is reminiscent of morality plays. This is evident, for example, in season 2 of *Breaking Bad* which opens with the image of a child's pink bear, floating in a swimming pool – everything else shown in grayscale.[1] The bear is missing an eyeball and appears to be completely burnt on one side. The motif foreshadows the events of the season 2 finale: a midair collision between a Boeing 737 and a noncommercial airliner.[2] This proves to be the mistake of an individual air traffic controller, racked with grief over the heroin-related asphyxiation of his daughter,[3] which Walter witnessed but chose not to prevent.[4] The child's bear is apparently debris from the crashed aircraft. Its eye is detached, but the missing eye resurfaces repeatedly throughout the following season, as if to suggest divine judgement. The aircraft collision, meanwhile, is emblematic of those closest

---

1   'Seven Thirty Seven'. *Breaking Bad*. American Movie Classics. AMC, New York City. 8 Mar. 2009. Television.
2   'ABQ'. *Breaking Bad*. American Movie Classics. AMC, New York City. 31 May 2009. Television.
3   Ibid.
4   'Phoenix'. *Breaking Bad*. American Movie Classics. AMS, New York City. 24 May 2009. Television.

to Walter (at this point, Skyler has taken their children and left him). The sequence is perhaps far-fetched, but the message it delivers is clear: characters in *Breaking Bad* are unable to escape the ramifications of their crimes.

Perhaps one of the morality play's most prominent tropes is the representative nature of its characters. These characters are personifications of such attributes as 'justice' and 'equity'.[5] *Breaking Bad* does quite parallel this tendency where, for example, in *Mundus et Infans* the protagonist is named Manhood, representing all of humanity.[6] Names such as Walter, Jesse and Skyler may seem relatively banal, but each character in the television drama personifies different values. For example, the supporting character of Jesse Pinkman embodies innocence. He is Walter's protégé and he draws much sympathy from viewers. In the latter half of *Breaking Bad*, Walter's transformation is nearing completion: he seems to revel in his power and 'the empire business'.[7] It is Jesse, a longstanding, petty felon who wishes to withdraw from criminal life.[8] The initial premise of *Breaking Bad* is that Walter, an innocuous schoolteacher, enters into a life of crime to which he is unsuited and descends into villainy. In fact, viewers learn that it is Jesse who is unfit for the immoral life. Arguably, nothing provokes Jesse's concern more than the death of Drew Sharp. Drew Sharp is a child who is witness to Walter and Jesse stealing chemicals from a train.[9] The child is fatally shot by Todd Alquist, a minor character, and Jesse is later haunted by the event. Walter, however, is seen to be whistling,[10] which Jesse interprets as callousness. Jesse's moral agency—juxtaposed against Walter's lack of conscience—shows that he is indeed the incarnation of the innocent.

Given the five or six centuries separating the prominence of morality plays and television dramas such as *Breaking Bad*, it is not surprising that they have significant differences. The goal of morality plays was to proselytise. In *Breaking Bad*, morality is made clear in its themes and symbolism, but viewers are never unambiguously directed to differentiate right from wrong. Moreover, although *Breaking Bad* contains intertextual religious allusion, it treats the afterlife quite differently from morality plays.

In *The Summoning of the Everyman*, the story is centred entirely on Everyman's struggle to cross to the afterlife with a clear conscience. Morality plays would not be what they are without the unquestionable faith in an afterlife. This contrasts with Walter who, in word and deed, has no faith in an afterlife. Walter's plan is to cook crystal methamphetamine in an effort to leave his wife and children a sufficient amount of money after he dies from lung cancer. Walter does not think beyond this. This is vividly highlighted in season 3 in the episode called 'Fly',[11] in which Walter and Jesse commit to removing a housefly that has entered their laboratory. In one shot, the camera looks down on the characters, apparently in judgement of them. However, Jesse is positioned closer to the camera, apparently above Walter, and thus symbolised as (more) innocent. Jesse attempts to swat the fly, but fails to succeed—he cannot swat a fly—as Walter drifts out of consciousness, succumbing to a sedative Jessie has given him. Walter reflects that he has lived too long, and searches his memory for what might have been a perfect moment to die. The first criterion is that he 'had to have enough [money]… none of this makes sense if [he] didn't have enough'.[12] Secondly, 'it had to be before [Skyler] found out'.[13] However, at this point, Skyler has discovered the truth, so Walter cannot untether himself from his earthbound wrongdoings.

5   Appelbaum, Stanley, and Ward, Candice, eds. *Everyman and Other Miracle & Morality Plays*. New York: Dover Publications, Inc, 1995. Print.
6   Lester, G.A. ed. *Three Late Medieval Morality Plays: Everyman, Mankind, and Mundus et Infans*. London: A&C Black Publishers Limited, 1990. Print.
7   'Buyout'. *Breaking Bad*. American Movie Classics. AMC, New York City. 19 Aug. 2012. Television.
8   Ibid.
9   'Dead Freight'. *Breaking Bad*. American Movie Classics. AMC, New York City. 12 Aug. 2012. Television.
10 Ibid.
11 'Fly'. *Breaking Bad*. American Movie Classics. AMC, New York City. 23 May 2010. Television.
12 Ibid.
13 Ibid.

Instead, his cancer is in remission and there is 'no end in sight'.[14] Walter's wish to die at a particular point of time is reflected in his obsessive fixation on the housefly, symbolically a 'fly in the ointment' of his master plan. Moreover, Walter's desire demonstrates his undying faith in science, and his need to 'respect the chemistry'.[15] While characters and audiences of morality plays aspire to an afterlife, Walter is preoccupied only with his lived life.

It is not surprising that *Breaking Bad* and morality plays differ, although sharing certain conventions. They exist in different eras and forms, and their audiences and purposes also differ. Where morality plays were concerned with proselytisation, *Breaking Bad* is concerned with art. *Breaking Bad* captivates viewers with morally ambiguous stories. Walter's misdeeds and their consequences leave viewers to determine who is good and bad, and it is this that fundamentally separates morality plays from *Breaking Bad*. *Breaking Bad*s' creator and executive producer, Vince Gilligan argues that his ultimate motivation was always to 'make people who they're pulling for, and why'.[16]

Works cited

Appelbaum, Stanley, and Ward, Candice, eds. *Everyman and Other Miracle & Morality Plays*. New York: Dover Publications, Inc, 1995. Print.

Bowles, Scott. "Breaking Bad' shows man at his worst in season 4.' USA Today. Gannet Co. Inc., 13 Jul. 2011. Web. 27 Feb. 2020.

Breaking Bad: The Complete Series. Writ. Sam Caitlin et al. High Bridge Entertainment, Gran Via Productions, Sony Pictures Television, 2008-2013. Blu-Ray.

Lester, G.A. ed. *Three Late Medieval Morality Plays: Everyman, Mankind, and Mundus et Infans*. London: A&C Black Publishers Limited, 1990. Print.

---

14 Ibid.

15 'Más'. *Breaking Bad*. American Movie Classics. AMC, New York City. 18 Apr. 2010. Television.

16 Bowles, Scott. "*Breaking Bad*' shows man at his worst in season 4.' USA Today. Gannet Co. Inc., 13 Jul 2011. Web. 27 Feb. 2020.

Sample HL essay 2

How do Emily Dickinson's poems present a personal challenge to move beyond conventional modes of thought to support her journey to self-knowledge and introspection?

Emily Dickinson challenges herself to think beyond conventional norms and charts the different intellectual rungs she must climb to attain self-knowledge. In 'I cannot live without You' and 'He fumbles at your Soul', she explores the ways in which her lover and an unknown deity curtail her emotional independence. In a similar vein, in 'Because I could not stop for Death' and 'I felt a Funeral in my Brain', Dickinson meditates on death and bereavement to adopt an overwhelmingly existentialist perspective; in comparison, 'There's a certain Slant of Light' documents her negativity in a religious context.

Criterion C: line of enquiry well developed from the start

Criterion D: language well chosen and precise

Dickinson's poems chart the significant emotional stages in her journey to introspection which challenge her to question conventional modes of thought with regard to human limitations, and the effect of controlling existences (her lover and God) on her beliefs. In 'I cannot live without You' Dickinson directly addresses her lover by declaring her physical and emotional reliance on him with a dissonant sense of underlying bitterness and gratitude. The verb 'live' in the title – literally describing the fundamental action of staying alive – is a primary necessity for all creatures, metaphorically suggesting that the addressee is essential for her emotional comfort and the purpose of her existence. The poem proceeds with the passionate pledge 'Were You lost, I would be- / Though my Name'. The personal pronouns are both capitalised to visually convey the closeness of the two lovers. Moreover, the structural dash is, in itself, a paradox, for its function is simultaneously to unite and separate the flow of two stanzas by aligning the unrelated arguments of her reliance and personal identity. By slicing the linearity of her own thought processes with her idiosyncratic punctuation, Dickinson presents her opposing internal conflict and inexorable confusion: her repulsion towards the toxic relationship on which, illogically, she is entirely dependent. The last stanza explores her response to the possibility of separation involving 'that White sustenance-/ Despair-'. White is conventionally attributed to the purity she could gain alone; however, in a negative vein it can also connote surrender. Despite the newly-found noble and healthy distance, 'sustenance' remains unrhymed, underscoring how it does not sufficiently nourish Dickinson to highlight her inescapable dependence on the addressee. Steven Cramer has convincingly argued that the formality of the rhyme scheme is ratcheted up in the final section. The couplet internally rhymes 'prayer' and 'despair' to portray the 'perfection of her argument in the poem's conclusion'. Furthermore, the rhymed words express the problem eloquently for 'prayer' could replace its synonym 'hope', for, in losing faith in the afterlife, she has replaced it

Criterion A: persuasive interpretation of the implication suggested by the text

Criterion B: insightful and convincing analysis of contextual features

with an earthly devotion: her lover. In a similar vein, the lyric 'He fumbles at your Soul' portrays the manipulation suffered by the poet by mirroring her submission to religious dogma and recognition of human irrelevance into the reader's perspective. The verb 'fumbles' carries the connotation of awkwardness, reflecting her personal insecurities and incompetence. Furthermore, the pronoun 'He' has an ambivalent refusal to be pinned down to a single entity and is a passive component of the sentence rather than an active one, conveying the unbalanced power dynamic between the subtended narrator and the deity. The poem also closes with a fall in emotional intensity when 'The Universe-is still-'. The last stanza could reflect a sense of abandonment and insignificance as, despite her previous epiphany, it continues to exist unaltered to convey her inconsequential nature (if the penultimate syllable is emphasised in reading). However, the stressed ultimate syllable could simultaneously register literal immobility to evoke uncertainty.

> **Criterion C:** supporting examples are well integrated

Dickinson is also able to fathom her most intimate fears and anxieties through her meditations on death's recurring haunting qualities. In the poem 'Because I could not stop for Death', Dickinson takes the reader on a metaphorical journey through and beyond time by charting her emotions during her parting from life in a carriage. The personification of 'Death' as a coachman humanises the event to register her welcoming appreciation of it. Her will to leave the land of the living is further portrayed by the narration of 'we passed the Setting Sun'. The metaphorical image connotes her passage into eternity for sunsets inexorably lead to darkness, a conventional euphemism for death. However, the soft sibilant sounds of 'Setting Sun' reflect the surprising tranquil and idyllic qualities of the calm scenery and, by implication, Dickinson's desire to undertake this rite of passage. However, there is an evident shift in temperament at the beginning of the fourth stanza when Dickinson realises 'Or rather - He passed us' for 'Only Gossamer my Gown'. The variation to a three-beat structure in 'He passed Us' carries a sinister connotation and the object pronoun 'He' (death) exerts control and dominance when overpassing Dickinson, marking the 'voltafaccia' in her emotional process from trusting to wary of death. The alliterative assonance in 'Gossamer' and 'Gown' draws attention to her inappropriate attire to convey the discomfort of having underestimated the bleakness of unforgiving eternity. Moreover, the silken and translucent texture of the material confers ethereal properties upon it and can metaphorically be read as an allusion to her spirit and soul released at the time of her death, both indexes of interior beliefs, to register Dickinson's achievement of introspection through this particular reflection. In a similar vein, the poem 'I Felt a Funeral in My Brain' conveys her grief when considering the all-pervasive notion of loss. The poet probes her emotions as 'A Service, like a Drum-' makes her 'mind' go 'numb'. The monosyllabic words act in conjunction with the auditory image as the all-consuming, monolithic sound of the instrument reduces the vastness of Dickinson's surroundings to concentrate on her emotional interiority. The perfect rhyme between the two terms (drum; numb) conveys the consequence of her reflections on funeral services on her mental health, by aurally linking them together.

> **Criterion C:** well developed line of enquiry

> **Criterion B:** insightful and convincing analysis of textual features and the author's broader choices in relation to the topic

This is because numbness suggests disorientation, shock and an inability to perceive feelings in a normative manner, remaining emotionally constrained by her contemplations on bereavement.

Dickinson further examines her personal nihilistic view on conventionally positive beliefs by recording her melancholia in the oppressive setting of a church and its environs. The poem 'There's a Certain Slant of Light' recounts her individual experience when attending a sermon, and describes a ray of light seeping through a stained-glass window from her pessimistic perspective. The title itself describes the beam with a laser-like intensity which is supposedly able to pass without scarring its surroundings, yet this image of extreme beauty evokes existentialist thoughts in the mind of the poet, and triggers the following acknowledgement of her dark vision of the world. Furthermore, Dickinson situates the event in 'winter afternoons'. The pathetic fallacy here registers her miserable and dejected outlook as the compound noun depicts a stagnant and cold location. The plurality of 'afternoons' is particularly interesting for it suggests that this is a repeated occurrence rather than a single event to portray the poet's frequent negativity. In addition, the second line of this rhyming couplet proceeds to explain that the light 'oppresses, like the Heft/ of Cathedral Tunes'. The simile directly compares the perceived domination of the light to that of religious hymns, bearing a spiritual connotation. Dickinson does not openly link the music to sacred choruses, but the two adjacent terms 'tunes' and 'cathedral' convey her interpretation of religion as a daunting and all-consuming stigma. Moreover, although the primary function of 'Heft' is that of a noun, its homogenous meaning as a verb registers a coarse physical effort, as well as the successful act of lifting. Dickinson evidently perceives traditionally enriching music as a metaphorical weight, and it is the oxymoron which gives the image its synergy to portray the unexpected burden of faith. Therefore, this troubling reckoning with God and religious suppression effectively conveys the fundamental motive for Dickinson's poetry: her puritan intent of recording profound and paradoxical thought processes which, in this particular poem, deconstruct the accepted perception of the benign celestial existence. In a similar vein, the penultimate stanza of 'Because I could not stop for Death' deflates the expectation of a bucolic heavenly scenario by depicting a 'House' in which the 'Roof was scarcely visible'. This metaphorical representation of a grave has damp and suffocating connotations in which her human body will rot for eternity. However, its ultimate significance as a home, an index of comfort and serenity, conveys her regret of having been falsely lured by the security of mortality and promise of an infinite afterlife.

It is through the process of writing these poems, therefore, that Dickinson is able to conjure existentialist thoughts and contemplate the insignificance of humanity as a whole, as well as on the weakness of her character. In each one, the poet achieves and charts an emotional epiphany, having reached a conclusive though often ambiguous realisation, and questions the fundamental notions of religion, death and human restraints, which paradoxically hinder her from further overcoming conventional boundaries.

Criterion C: supporting examples well integrated in the text

Criterion C: well developed line of enquiry

6

Sample HL essay 3

How does Carol Ann Duffy highlight the power dynamics that exist between married couples, in her collection *The World's Wife*?

In her collection, The World's Wife, Duffy examines marital tensions and their complex dynamics. She explores societal expectations of married couples, inequality within sexual relationships, and almost as a counterpoint to these tensions, the tempering power of genuine love. We find a clue in the titles: 'Pygmalion's Bride', 'Mrs Lazarus,' 'Mrs Midas' and 'Mrs Faust'. All these titles relegate women to the role of 'Mrs' or 'Bride': subjugated, dependent, certainly not entities in and of themselves. In essence, Duffy is conveying the disparity that lies at the heart of these relationships, forcefully making the point that it is men who are, while not exclusively, predominantly to blame for the perpetuation of an enduring patriarchal society.

Duffy critiques the repressive impact of societal conventions and gender roles on relationships. 'Pygmalion's Bride', taking inspiration from the Greek myth of the sculptor Pygmalion, presents a man courting a woman with 'pebbles and little things', graduating to 'pearls, necklaces and rings'. This depicts a commonly accepted 'truth' that the affections of a woman can be bought. By pluralising the inducements ('necklaces' and 'rings'), Duffy implies the predatory determination of the man to obtain the object of his desire. The woman remains 'shtum' while he runs his 'clammy hands' along her limbs – the adjective 'clammy' imbuing a sense of disgust, which is juxtaposed with her implied acquiescence. It ends in his conquest and subsequent abandonment of the woman, with the bride ending the poem with a perhaps falsely blasé utterance: 'Haven't seen him since/ Simple as that'. These two short lines convey that either the woman is unconcerned, or, more likely, is feigning indifference after being jilted. The repeated use of sibilance suggests the words being bitterly spat out. Comparably, 'Mrs Lazarus' explores the convention at the other end of a relationship's lifecycle; a further patriarchal notion that society expects a widow to remain faithful after her husband's death. This is supported by an almost taboo image of the widow being a 'gaunt nun ... touching herself', equating the grieving woman to a harrowed and sex-starved 'nun' who has to resort to sinful activities. Compounding society's disapprobation, 'the sly light on the blacksmith's face' and 'the shrill eyes of the barmaid' give everyday individuals a menacing mien through the clever adjectival use of 'sly' and 'shrill', as they both communicate negative connotations. This illustrates the societal obligation for Mrs Lazarus to take back her 'bridegroom in his rotting shroud', demonstrating society's belief that a woman is a chattel to be handed back to her owner, no matter how unpleasant and putrid he may be. Lum powerfully asserts that 'no one should be subject to this kind of trauma' because, as she puts it, 'marriage is . . . a contract that is . . . broken by death'. This supports Duffy's intent to highlight a situation that is not just unfair, but which makes the point that Mrs Lazarus's opinion is of no

Criterion C: well organised and cohesive

Criterion C: introduction effectively organised and has a clear thesis statement

Criterion B: convincing analysis of plurality and its effect

Criterion B: effective use of text to support the argument

Criterion B: evaluation of different textual techniques

Criterion A: well-chosen quotations

Criterion C: organised conclusion is reached

consequence. Here Duffy is reflecting a reality which is pertinent to many contemporary women. Similarly, the subject of sexual relations is explored by Duffy to present the unreasonable expectations that men have of women, and the unappealing, and even threatening, effect an empowered woman can have on men. Despite the woman describing her sexual fervour as 'all an act' in 'Pygmalion's Bride', Duffy's description renders this unconvincing. The alliteration and pithiness of the phrase 'all an act' give a sense of finality. However, the woman is depicted to warm 'like candle wax' – a sensuous simile, relating to the texture of a woman's skin and revealing the potential implication of something dangerous, capable of causing damage. The woman's passion is viscerally illustrated through the fact that she 'coiled' and 'writhed'. This frantic, animalistic series of descriptions, using serpent-like actions, work together to display her passionate reaction to the event and contradict her denial of enjoyment. Duffy is reflecting on a truism with regards to sexual relations: the notion that men desire what they cannot obtain. When the woman is a statue, and Pygmalion's love is unrequited, he labours for her attention. Conversely, when she becomes responsive, she loses her mystique in Pygmalion's eyes. The fact that she 'hasn't seen him since', succinctly sums up a typical loss of interest once the man has obtained the object of his desire. Similarly, 'Mrs Faust' presents a man's loss of interest in his wife as a result of her own empowerment. The issue of loss of attraction is prominent; Faust grows to 'love the kudos, not the wife', showing that he is far more concerned with the affection and praise he receives from society than romantic love from his wife. Duffy adopts a ballad structure in 'Mrs Faust' which is apt, given her storytelling perspective. The narrative nature of the poem is complemented by the lyrical tone, thus drawing her audience in. Faust's degeneration, leading to him visiting 'whores', further alludes to his loss of interest in his wife, arguably as she is 'just as bad' as he. Duffy appears to be suggesting that a woman who ceases to be an acquisition, but rather an affluent equal to her husband, holds no further attraction to him.

Duffy, through her focus on oppression, sometimes verging on domestic abuse, presents a fundamental imbalance in power within marital relationships, with the man usually holding sway. The most evident display of this is in 'Pygmalion's Bride', where the 'stone-cool' wife has literally been created by the man. Purity and frigidity are simultaneously portrayed by Duffy. By studying the poem from a chromatic perspective, 'ivory' and 'snow' are both white, typically a colour relating to purity, and so it can be interpreted that Pygmalion is exploiting her innocence. The mention of 'cold' and 'stone-cool lips' is also highly suggestive of a woman who has no interest in sexual intimacy. The poem descends into a disturbing portrayal of exploitative seduction. Duffy indicates an obvious display of masculine ownership when Pygmalion 'look[s] for marks' on his bride's skin. This shows his need for tangible evidence of ownership. He searches 'for purple hearts, for inky stars, for smudgy clues' – referring to bruises, insinuating lustful intentions. Duffy does not content herself with just one description of what could only be called Pygmalion's abuse; she uses no fewer than three metaphors to describe the bruising. The first two verge on the jarringly

Criterion D: carefully chosen language with a high degree of accuracy

Criterion C: well-integrated example to support argument

Criterion C: clear argument stated

Criterion C: line of enquiry is well developed

Criterion B: analysis is clear and effective

oxymoronic, entailing injuries in the shape of hearts and stars; however, the final metaphor reveals the uncomfortable truth: that he has 'smudg[ed]' his bride, leaving 'clues' – things commonly associated with crimes. A further interpretation of the act of 'smudg[ing]' is that in defacing the statue, Pygmalion metaphorically defiles her and consequently diminishes her worth.

Interestingly, Duffy extends her exploration of sexual politics beyond exclusively male oppression within marriage. Horner points out that in fact both sexes are 'damaged by [forms of patriarchy] in different ways'. In 'Mrs Midas', Duffy turns the idea of male dominance on its head. Her portrayal of an uxorious 'fool' of a husband, compelled to live in a 'caravan in the wilds' is an example of a marital relationship where the wife is the dominant power. The monosyllabic sentence 'so he had to move out', demonstrates the blunt nonchalance with which she dismisses her husband. Midas's wife does not hold back, accusing her husband of 'pure selfishness' and a blatant 'lack of thought' for her. This conveys not just her bitterness, but also expresses a certain sense of superiority over her husband or, as Lanone appropriately notes, 'the empowered wife is saved by common sense'. This reinforces the contention that Mrs Midas acknowledges the danger that lies in continuing to pursue a relationship with her husband, and in doing so, demonstrates her superior judgement. Despite Duffy's presentation of resentment and power imbalance between married couples, she also depicts tender elements within certain relationships. 'Mrs Lazarus' portrays the utter sorrow that is the result of loss, thus showing us another side of power imbalance; how delicate power balances can be upset through physical loss. In the first stanza, the series of stressed, monosyllabic verbs ('howled, shrieked, clawed, retched') replicate cries of anguish, revealing how bereft the woman is without her husband. The widow's bereavement is presented through the metaphor that accompanies her self-description of being 'one empty glove', signifying that she has lost a partner in life, as one glove is forlorn and useless without the other. This melancholy act of grieving conveys the existence of love, however impotent, even after death. Likewise, 'Mrs Faust' gives a conflicted account of how an unequal relationship can shift towards one of greater equality. Despite their predominantly separate lives, the pair appear to see eye to eye. The repetition of the pronoun 'we' represents the harmony within the relationship. In the final stanza, Mrs Faust recounts how she 'keep[s] Faust's secret still' and that 'the clever, cunning, callous bastard didn't have a soul to sell'. The repetition of the harsh 'c's along with the softer alliteration of 'soul to sell' give an almost lyrical tone to the lines, despite their harsh message. It seems plausible that she uses this tone, along with the description 'bastard', in a begrudgingly affectionate way. This presents their mutual understanding, and a degree of fondness in their soulless unity.

Duffy presents the inequality within relationships by examining the impact of society, the act of sexual relations and the oppression of predominantly females, but also males. Examination of her poetry reveals that she does not adopt a binary approach when exploring marital relationships. She revels in the complexity of human relations, counter-balancing lust with affection, novelty with familiarity and conflicting positions of power. Duffy's themes are age-old and immutable. It is no coincidence that she chooses wives of characters from ancient texts to make the reader think about just how applicable these marital relations are to those around us in the present day. Equally, the title of her collection of poems, The World's Wife, is both paradoxical and significant. On the one hand, women are shown to be subjugated to their husbands, but to be the wife of the world, like Hera, is to have an elemental and unassailable power.

Sample HL essay 4

How does Dickinson's refusal to accept that she doesn't 'fit in' drive her explorations of suffering across time in her poetry?

For Dickinson, 'not fitting in' is the ever-present pain that follows her through the different spheres of her life. She is anguished by her seeming separation that she feels between her current state and her archetypic expectation of herself, but she also feels dejected and estranged from the society surrounding her, feeling like a spectator to the movement she is inevitably exposed to. The apotheosis of her dissociation is her neglect in the eyes of God, resentful and confused as to why she is treated this way.

Dickinson's feelings of 'not fitting in' derive initially from her cognitive dissonance, the distance and contradiction between her consciousness, and the version of herself she wishes to be. We are confronted with her separation from herself in 'I tried to think a lonelier thing'. She tells of a journey to finding the ultimate form of loneliness. In the fourth stanza she describes her attempts at overcoming the barrier between her two selves. She states that 'I plucked at our Partition/ … Between Himself – and Horror's Twin –'. One reading of this could entail that she is referring to herself when she speaks of 'Horror's Twin'. She sees herself as a manifestation of the traditionally gothic semantic term 'Horror' and is plucking, searching for the better version of herself. The lexical choice of the verb 'plucked' in the past tense is useful when parsing Dickinson's suffering. 'Plucked' denotes a repeated, sharp, physically very painful form of suffering, and the usage of the past tense implies that Dickinson has given up – arguably because this pain was too unbearable, she is ultimately unable to leave 'Horror' behind. We also feel this physical separation in 'I cannot live with You –', where the conclusive stanza resolves that 'We must meet apart – / You there – I – here'. The dashes that surround the personal pronoun 'I' are a physical representation of the phrase 'We must meet apart'. The dash visually separates and isolates the narrator but is also a link between the two notional locations. This poem is usually read as a love poem, and critics such

> Criterion A: good understanding and knowledge of the work

as Lillian Faderman mistakenly interpret Dickinson's lyrics as 'homoerotic'. It could also be seen as, indeed, a love poem, but in the less traditional sense, where the impossible love is between Dickinson and the version of herself she longs to be, the one she sees perfect in her eyes. There is a sense of detachment from life itself, namely in 'It was not Death, for I stood up' where the opening line adopts an apophatic method of enquiry, denoting what the things she is experiencing are not, resulting in the assumption that she is referring to life itself. However, she is observing it and analysing it from a paradoxical outsider's point of view. Despite her experiencing the things first-hand, as registered by her use of the personal pronoun 'I', she describes everything almost as if she were watching herself go through the motions. Her description of what the things she sees are not, gives the impression she herself cannot truly experience life – she feels detached, not fitting in her own body, resulting in constant despair. It is also interesting to note her disregard for the convention of giving poems titles. Each of her poems is referred to by their first line. This unwillingness to give a poem a name could be a representation of her struggle to define herself and her state. Aligning to the perception she holds of herself, each one of her poems has multiple separate sides and focal points – thus, by giving a title one would be prioritised over the other.

Dickinson's 'not fitting in' extends from her deep personal perception of herself, seeping into her social circumstances. Her depiction of her isolation and resultant feelings of lonely suffering are presented in 'It was not death, for I stood up'. As she describes and discusses a funeral, she states that it 'Reminded me, of mine –'. this is clearly paradoxical, seeing as by the very nature of the poetry she is indeed biologically alive. This implication that she is not living adds another layer to the sense of observation of her own life, now placing herself as an observer of the lives of others. While they are living, she feels dead, a significantly different state. It carries a sense of superiority towards those she is watching, as presented in the phrase 'The Figures I have seen', almost as if the first and most important quality to consider when describing the figures is that she has seen them. Her clinging on to death–almost disturbed by the fact someone from the world she feels so alienated from is now joining her in the place she feels like she belongs in–is reflected in the lexical choice of the possessive adjective 'mine –'. The separation between her and the people around her is emphasised by the unconventional dash, which Dickinson uses to build a wall, a physical separation between the narrative voice and her surroundings. Her sense of 'not fitting in' are also emphasised in the phrase that follows, where she feels 'As if my life were shaven/ And fitted to a key'. We can infer her feelings of violation from the verb 'shaven', which has a connotation of a precise, definite change of an entity's shape. The idea of this being done to someone's life is quite disturbing. This is then further emphasised by the image of the 'key', the nature of a key being that it is somehow required to enter a space, and is reflected in her own personal narrative – she needs a 'key' in order to access the rest of society she feels so alienated from.

Criterion B: consistently insightful, and a convincing analysis

Criterion C: essay is effectively organised and cohesive

Criterion C: example is well integrated

Criterion A: persuasive implications shown, and understanding of the work is shown as well

Finally, Dickinson's sense of 'not fitting in' culminates in her feeling of rejection, neglect, and being ignored by God. In her poem 'I took one draught of Life–' she describes an evaluation of her 'Being's worth', where she discusses the price she was forced to pay, simply for being alive. She tells how 'they weighed me, Dust by Dust'. This biblical allusion, referring to the famous phrase 'for dust thou art, and unto dust shalt thou return', is held up to critical analysis in her poem. She refers to it as a clinical, precise action, as alluded to by the use of the verb 'weighed', often used in scientific or precise procedures. Furthermore, she presents the reader with her sense of neglect by God himself. By using this Biblical phrase, she emphasises that she feels treated unfairly – man is 'Dust' before and after birth; she feels that during life humans are worth more. By comparing her state to that of 'Dust' she presents herself as dead. Although we do not know who she feels is evaluating her due to the indefinite pronoun 'they', we can assume that they are somehow linked to religion, but they are not God. This denotes Dickinson's impression that she is being delegated to someone else, as if God didn't deem her worthy enough of his attention and gave instructions that resulted in 'they handed me my being's worth – / A single Dram of Heaven'. The sense of worthlessness Dickinson experiences is emphasised further by the ambiguous noun 'Dram'. Its meanings of both a minuscule unit of weight, and a Scottish term for a small dose of spirit, allow us insight into this perception. The nature of an alcoholic beverage is quite interesting in this context; by giving it to Dickinson, it is almost as if 'they' are trying to distract her from the meagreness of what she is receiving, hampering her consciousness and judgement. She blames her suffering on this arguable mistreatment, following the logic that, if even God doesn't deem her worthy of anything more than a 'Dram', and sees her as mere 'Dust', her life might as well be over. This isolation from God is emphasised further in the aforementioned poem 'I tried to think a lonelier thing'. Here, in the opening stanza where she tells of her search for the loneliest entity in existence, she recounts her 'Polar Expiation'. Unlike the similar sounding term 'exploration', which would be the more naturally fitting term here, the connotation of the verb 'Expiation' is that of an act of reparation of guilt or wrongdoing. We can suspect Dickinson is exploring both extremes, as suggested by the adjective 'Polar', in order to find something she can apologise for in order to re-enter God's grace. This feeling of worthlessness is arguably what results in her suffering, seeing as the one realm of life and consciousness that is traditionally meant to stay stable during tough times, is now ignoring her.

In conclusion, the quest to find belonging, whether that be within our own mind and expectations, the society surrounding us, or the divine power we desperately seek, is presented by Dickinson as an inexorable part of the human condition. Dickinson especially demonstrates the effect that a lack of this sensation of belonging can have on the human condition, and one's experience of life. Her gruesome, raw emotion, the very core of her soul is covetous for belonging.

Criterion B: essay demonstrates a consistently insightful and convincing analysis and evaluation of textual features

Criterion D: clear and varied language

Paper 1: Guided textual analysis

Criterion A: Understanding and interpretation

What is assessed?

An understanding of the text – what is revealed and inferred – using supporting references.

Marks	Description of level
0	The response does not meet the standards described by the descriptors below.
1	There is little understanding of the surface meaning. The response seldom supports claims with evidence, or supporting evidence is seldom appropriate.
2	There is some understanding of the surface meaning. The response supports claims with evidence that is sometimes appropriate.
3	There is an understanding of the surface meaning and some inferential understanding. The response supports claims with evidence that is mainly relevant.
4	There is a detailed understanding of the surface meaning and a convincing inferential understanding. The response supports claims with relevant evidence.
5	There is a detailed and insightful understanding of surface meaning, and a convincing and nuanced inferential understanding. The response supports claims with well-selected evidence.

Criterion B: Analysis and evaluation

What is assessed?

An understanding of language, style and structure, and an ability to critically evaluate writers' choices to construct meaning.

Marks	Description of level
0	The response does not meet the standards described by the descriptors below.
1	There is little analysis of language and style to construct meaning. The commentary is descriptive.
2	There is some analysis of language and style to construct meaning. The commentary is mainly descriptive.
3	There is a mainly appropriate analysis of the ways in which language and style construct meaning. Some of the analysis is insightful.

Marks	Description of level
4	There is an appropriate analysis of the ways in which language and style construct meaning. Some of the analysis is insightful. There is some evaluation of how meaning is shaped by writers' choices.
5	There is an insightful and convincing analysis of the ways in which language and style construct meaning. There is very good evaluation of how meaning is shaped by writers' choices.

Criterion C: Focus and organisation

What is assessed?

An ability to organise ideas in a coherent and focused way.

Marks	Description of level
0	The response does not meet the standards described by the descriptors below.
1	There is little organisation and no obvious focus.
2	There is some organisation and a degree of focus.
3	There is adequate organisation, some coherence and some focus.
4	There is good organisation, a good degree of coherence and adequate focus.
5	There is effective organisation and coherence, and a good degree of focus.

Criterion D: Language

What is assessed?

An ability to write with clarity, accuracy and variety. An ability to write in an appropriate academic register. An ability to include relevant terminology where appropriate.

Marks	Description of level
0	The response does not meet the standards described by the descriptors below.
1	There is little clarity or accuracy. There is little sense of an appropriate register.
2	There is some clarity and accuracy. There is some sense of an appropriate register. Errors are apparent.

Marks	Description of level
3	There is adequate clarity and accuracy. The register is mainly appropriate. Some lapses are apparent.
4	There is good clarity and accuracy. The register is consistently appropriate.
5	There is very good clarity and accuracy, and a strong sense of precision. The register is consistently appropriate and effective.

Paper 2: Comparative essay

Criterion A: Knowledge, understanding and interpretation

What is assessed?

A knowledge and understanding of literary works. A response to the question that is relevant, showing similarities and differences in the works studied.

Marks	Description of level
0	The response does not meet the standards described by the descriptors below.
1–2	There is little knowledge and understanding of the works, and there is little comparison of the works in relation to the question.
3–4	There is limited knowledge and understanding of the works, and there is limited comparison of the works in relation to the question.
5–6	There is satisfactory knowledge and understanding of the works, and there is satisfactory comparison of the works in relation to the question.
7–8	There is good knowledge and understanding of the works, and there is relevant comparison of the works in relation to the question. The discussion is somewhat sustained.
9–10	There is very good knowledge and understanding of the works, and there is insightful comparison of the works in relation to the question. The discussion is sustained and insightful.

Criterion B: Analysis and evaluation

What is assessed?

An analysis and evaluation of language, technique and style to establish meaning and effect.
Through analysis and evaluation, appropriate similarities and differences are shown in response to
the question.

Marks	Description of level
0	The response does not meet the standards described by the descriptors below.
1–2	The response is descriptive, offering little relevant analysis.
3–4	The response is somewhat analytical, but mainly descriptive. There is limited comparison of writers' choices.
5–6	The response is generally analytical, offering some understanding of the ways in which language, technique and style establish meaning and effect. The response offers some insight, and there is some comparison of writers' choices.
7–8	The response is analytical and evaluative, offering understanding of the ways in which language, technique and style establish meaning and effect. There is a good comparison of writers' choices.
9–10	The response is analytical and evaluative, offering an insightful and convincing understanding of the ways in which language, technique and style establish meaning and effect. There is a good comparison of writers' choices.

Criterion C: Focus and organisation

What is assessed?

Structure, focus and balance.

Marks	Description of level
0	The response does not meet the standards described by the descriptors below.
1	There is limited focus, and the ideas are mainly unconnected.
2	There is some focus and some connection between ideas. Coherence may be inconsistent, and the discussion of works may lack balance.
3	There is mainly good focus despite some lapses. There is reasonable balance and a general sense of cohesion in the development of ideas.
4	There is a good focus that is largely maintained. There is good balance, and ideas develop consistently and logically.
5	There is a clear and consistent focus. There is very good balance, and ideas develop in a logical and compelling way.

Criterion D: Language

What is assessed?

An ability to write with clarity, accuracy and variety. An ability to write in an appropriate academic register. An ability to include relevant terminology where appropriate.

Marks	Description of level
0	The response does not meet the standards described by the descriptors below.
1	There is little clarity or accuracy. There is little sense of an appropriate register.
2	There is some clarity and accuracy. There is some sense of an appropriate register. Errors are apparent.
3	There is adequate clarity and accuracy. The register is mainly appropriate. Some lapses are apparent.
4	There is good clarity and accuracy. The register is consistently appropriate.
5	There is very good clarity and accuracy, and a strong sense of precision. The register is consistently appropriate and effective.

Individual oral

Criterion A: Knowledge, understanding and interpretation

What is assessed?

A knowledge and understanding of the extracts, and the wider works and texts from which they are taken. An application of this knowledge to the global issue chosen, drawing conclusions that are underpinned by reference to works and texts.

Marks	Description of level
0	The response does not meet the standards described by the descriptors below.
1–2	There is little knowledge and understanding of extracts, texts and works in the context of the global issue chosen. Supporting evidence is limited or inappropriate.
3–4	There is limited knowledge and understanding of extracts, texts and works in the context of the global issue chosen. Supporting evidence is sometimes appropriate.

Marks	Description of level
5–6	There is satisfactory knowledge and understanding of extracts, texts and works, offering an interpretation in the context of the global issue chosen. Supporting evidence is mainly appropriate and supports the development of ideas.
7–8	There is good knowledge and understanding of extracts, texts and works, offering a constant interpretation in the context of the global issue chosen. Supporting evidence is appropriate and supports the development of ideas.
9–10	There is excellent knowledge and understanding of extracts, texts and works, offering a compelling interpretation in the context of the global issue chosen. Supporting evidence is appropriate, carefully selected and supports the development of ideas.

Criterion B: Analysis and evaluation

What is assessed?

A knowledge and understanding of the extracts, and the wider works and texts from which they are taken, showing how writers' choices of language, structure and style construct and establish a perspective on the global issue chosen.

Marks	Description of level
0	The response does not meet the standards described by the descriptors below.
1–2	The oral is descriptive, or analysis is irrelevant. There is little discussion of language, structure and style in the context of the global issue chosen.
3–4	There is some relevant analysis, but this largely derives from description. Aspects of language, structure and style are highlighted, but understood only partially in the context of the global issue chosen.
5–6	There is analysis, revealing appropriate and evaluative commentary. There is reasonable understanding of language, structure and style in the context of the global issue chosen.
7–8	There is analysis, revealing appropriate and evaluative commentary that is at times insightful. There is good understanding of language, structure and style in the context of the global issue chosen.
9–10	There is analysis, revealing appropriate and evaluative commentary that is insightful. There is excellent and nuanced understanding of language, structure and style in the context of the global issue chosen.

Criterion C: Focus and organisation

What is assessed?

Structure, focus and balance. The ability to connect ideas coherently.

Marks	Description of level
0	The response does not meet the standards described by the descriptors below.
1–2	There is little focus, and ideas are rarely connected.
3–4	There is some focus, but there may be a lack of balance in how works and texts are discussed.
5–6	There is focus, but this may lapse. There may be a lack of balance in how works and texts are discussed. Connections are established between ideas, but not always coherently.
7–8	The oral is mainly clear and sustained. There is balance in how works and texts are discussed. Ideas develop consistently and coherently. The presentation of ideas is convincing.
9–10	The oral is mainly clear and sustained. There is good balance in how works and texts are discussed. The presentation of ideas is logical and convincing, connecting ideas insightfully.

Criterion D: Language

What is assessed?

Clarity and accuracy of language.

Marks	Description of level
0	The response does not meet the standards described by the descriptors below.
1–2	There is a general lack of clarity and precision. Aspects of style are inappropriate.
3–4	There is general clarity. Errors may affect communication. Errors are frequent. Aspects of style are often inappropriate.
5–6	There is clarity. Errors do not affect communication. Vocabulary and sentence structure are appropriate, but lack variation and sophistication. Aspects of style are appropriate.
7–8	There is clarity and accuracy. There may be small errors, but these do not affect communication. Vocabulary and sentence structure are appropriate and varied. Aspects of style are appropriate and may enhance the oral.

Marks	Description of level
9–10	There is clarity, accuracy and variation. There may be small errors, but these do not affect communication. Vocabulary and sentence structure are appropriate and varied, and enhance the presentation of ideas. Aspects of style are appropriate and enhance the oral.

Higher-level (HL) essay

Criterion A: Knowledge, understanding and interpretation

What is assessed?

A knowledge and understanding of literary works or texts, using appropriate supporting references to make inferences and draw conclusions relevant to the chosen focus.

Marks	Description of level
0	The response does not meet the standards described by the descriptors below.
1	There is little knowledge and understanding of the works or texts relevant to the chosen focus. There are few references to the works or texts, or references are mainly inappropriate.
2	There is some knowledge and understanding of the works or texts relevant to the chosen focus. There are some references to the works or texts, and these are sometimes appropriate.
3	There is a satisfactory knowledge and understanding of the works or texts relevant to the chosen focus. References to the works or texts are mainly relevant, and mainly support claims and arguments.
4	There is a good knowledge and understanding of the works or texts relevant to the chosen focus. Claims and arguments are sustained, and references support these claims and arguments.
5	There is excellent knowledge and understanding of the works or texts relevant to the chosen focus. Claims and arguments are persuasive, and references are well chosen, effectively supporting these claims and arguments.

Criterion B: Analysis and evaluation

What is assessed?

An analysis and evaluation of language, technique and style to establish meaning and effect relevant to the chosen topic.

Marks	Description of level
0	The response does not meet the standards described by the descriptors below.
1	The response is descriptive, offering little analysis relevant to the chosen topic.
2	The response is somewhat analytical, but is mainly descriptive relevant to the chosen topic.
3	The response is generally analytical, offering some understanding of the ways in which language, technique and style establish meaning and effect relevant to the chosen topic.
4	The response is analytical and evaluative, offering understanding of the ways in which language, technique and style establish meaning and effect relevant to the chosen topic.
5	The response is analytical and evaluative, offering an insightful and convincing understanding of the ways in which language, technique and style establish meaning and effect relevant to the chosen topic.

Criterion C: Focus, organisation and development

What is assessed?

Structure, focus, balance and the integration of examples.

Marks	Description of level
0	The response does not meet the standards described by the descriptors below.
1	There is little organisation. A sense of enquiry is not apparent. Supporting examples are not embedded into the essay.
2	There is some organisation. The line of enquiry lacks development. Supporting examples are rarely embedded into the essay.
3	There is adequate organisation and general cohesion. The line of enquiry shows some development. Supporting examples are sometimes embedded into the essay.
4	There is good organisation and the essay is mostly cohesive. The line of enquiry is mainly well developed. Supporting examples are mostly well embedded into the essay.
5	There is effective organisation and the essay is cohesive. The line of enquiry is well developed. Supporting examples are well embedded into the essay.

Criterion D: Language

What is assessed?

An ability to write with clarity, accuracy and variety. An ability to write in an appropriate academic register. An ability to include relevant terminology where appropriate.

Marks	Description of level
0	The response does not meet the standards described by the descriptors below.
1	There is little clarity or accuracy. There is little sense of an appropriate register.
2	There is some clarity and accuracy. There is some sense of an appropriate register. Errors are apparent.
3	There is adequate clarity and accuracy. The register is mainly appropriate. Some lapses are apparent.
4	There is good clarity and accuracy. The register is consistently appropriate.
5	There is very good clarity and accuracy, and a strong sense of precision. The register is consistently appropriate and effective.

Acknowledgements

The authors and publishers acknowledge the following sources of copyright material and are grateful for the permissions granted. While every effort has been made, it has not always been possible to identify the sources of all the material used, or to trace all copyright holders. If any omissions are brought to our notice, we will be happy to include the appropriate acknowledgements on reprinting.

Section 1 Excerpt and illustrations from *Salt, Fat, Acid, Heat* used by permission of Canongate Books Ltd. Copyright © Samin Nosrat, 2017. Illustrations © Wendy MacNaughton, 2017; Cartoon 'The Set Text' by Tom Gauld used with the permission of author; 'The Last to See Them Alive' from *IN COLD BLOOD* by Truman Capote, copyright © 1965 by Truman Capote and renewed 1993 by Alan U. Schwartz. Used by permission of Random House, an imprint and division of Penguin Random House LLC. All rights reserved; 'Wealthy Farmer, 3 Of Family Slain' publishef by The New York Times, 16 November 1959; An extract about '*We Transfer*' used with permission of We Transfer; Photo by Daniel Bevan/Alamy Stock Photo; Quote from WeTransfer used with permission of WeTransfer; Illustration used with permission of Cognitive Media and WeTransfer; Photo by GREGORY CREWDSON, Untitled, 2006, Digital pigment print, © Gregory Crewdson. Courtesy Gagosian; Pages from Wikipedia: Why Wikipedia is so great; **Section 2** 'Because I could not Stop for Death' by Emily Dickinson from *THE POEMS OF EMILY DICKINSON*, edited by Thomas H. Johnson, Cambridge, Mass.: The Belknap Press of Harvard University Press, Copyright © 1951, 1955 by the President and Fellows of Harvard College. Copyright © renewed 1979, 1983 by the President and Fellows of Harvard College. Copyright © 1914, 1918, 1919, 1924, 1929, 1930, 1932, 1935, 1937, 1942, by Martha Dickinson Bianchi. Copyright © 1952, 1957, 1958, 1963, 1965, by Mary L. Hampson; 'Mrs Lazarus' from *The World's Wife* by Carol Ann Duffy (Picador, 2017) Reproduced with permission of the Licensor through PLSclear; **Section 3** Quote © Musée du Louvre used with permission; Extracts from 'Julian Barnes Looks At Art' by Cody Delistraty, The New Yorker, October 14 2015 used with permission of Condé Nast; Quote from 'Photography: is it art?' Copyright Guardian News & Media Ltd 2020; Excerpt *'Keeping an Eye Open: Essays on Art'* by Julian Barnes, published by Jonathan Cape, a division of Penguin Random House UK; p98 photo Sergey Ponomarev/New York Times/Redux/eyevine; Images of Blake poems by Granger Historical Picture Archive/Alamy stock Photo, Artokoloro/Alamy Stock Photo, The Picture Art Collection/Alamy Stock Photo; **Section 4** '*What Kind of Times Are These*'. Copyright © 2016 by the Adrienne Rich Literary Trust. Copyright © 1995 by Adrienne Rich, from *COLLECTED POEMS: 1950--2012* by Adrienne Rich. Used by permission of W.W. Norton & Company, Inc; Excerpt(s) from *THE PEOPLE VS TECH: HOW THE INTERNET IS KILLING DEMOCRACY (AND HOW WE SAVE IT)* by Jamie Bartlett, copyright © 2018 by James Bartlett. Used by permission of Dutton, an imprint of Penguin Publishing Group, a division of Penguin Random House LLC & Penguin Random House UK, All rights reserved; Thunberg, Greta: speech on climate change to COP24 12th December 2018, Poland - published in *No one is too small to make a difference* by Greta Thunberg, reproduced with the permission of Penguin Random House UK, All rights reserved; Interview with Amy Chua by Hannah Hodson, Janusary 2011, Copyright Guardian News & Media Ltd 2020; **Section 5** 'Join the school strike for climate change' © Greenpeace, used with the permission; 'This is thrilling life-extension news – for dictators and the ultra-rich' by George Monbiot for the Guardian, July 2014, Copyright Guardian News & Media Ltd 2020; *"Crazy Rich Asians'* Review' in Empire, reproduced with the permission of H BAUER PUBLISHING; Photo by Spencer Platt/Getty Images

Thanks to Getty Images for permission to reproducethe following images:

Cover: Sean Gladwell; Section 1 Trevor Williams; Section 2 Thorsten Gast; Section 3 PeopleImages; Section 4 Hill Street Studios; Section 5 caiaimages; Section 6 jacoblund

We would like to thank the staff and students of Impington Village College for their time, effort and collaboration working with us on the Individual Oral recordings. Special thanks to Sonia Trickey for managing this with her class and to Jo Sale for allowing this to happen!